# Songs of the Green Hills

An Anthology of Korean Sijos

# Songs of the Green Hills

## An Anthology of Korean Sijos

Compiled by Kim Ch'ŏnt'aek

Translated by
Won-Chung Kim and Christopher Merrill

Introduction by In Sook Jeong

Homa & Sekey Books
Paramus, New Jersey

FIRST EDITION

Copyright © 2025 by Homa & Sekey Books
English translation copyright © 2025 by Won-Chung Kim and Christopher Merrill
Cover art: Chae Jongki

All rights reserved. No part of this book may be reproduced, stored in a retrieval system, or transmitted in any form, or by any means, electronic, mechanical, photocopying, recording or otherwise, without prior permission from the publisher.

Library of Congress Cataloging-in-Publication Data

Names: Kim, Ch'ŏnt'aek, active 1728, compiler. | Kim, Won-Chung, 1959- translator. | Merrill, Christopher, translator.
Title: Songs of the Green Hills: an Anthology of Korean Sijos / [compiled by Ch'ŏnt'aek Kim] translated by Won-Chung Kim and Christopher Merrill; introduction by In Sook Jeong.
Other titles: Ch'ŏnggu yŏngŏn. English
Description: First edition. | Paramus : Homa & Sekey Books, 2025. |
Identifiers: LCCN 2024040495 | ISBN 9781622461240 (paperback)
Subjects: LCSH: Sijo--Translations into English. | Korean poetry--Translations into English. | Korean poetry--To 1900.
Classification: LCC PL975.83 .K513 2025 | DDC 898.809519--dc23/eng/20240903
LC record available at https://lccn.loc.gov/2024040495

Published by Homa & Sekey Books
3rd Floor, North Tower
Mack-Cali Center III
140 E. Ridgewood Ave.
Paramus, NJ 07652

Tel: 201-261-8810; 800-870-HOMA
Fax: 201-261-8890
Email: info@homabooks.com
Website: www.homabooks.com

Printed in the U.S.A.
1 3 5 7 9 10 8 6 4 2

# Acknowledgements

This work was supported by the English Translation of 100 Korean Classics program through the Ministry of Education of the Republic of Korea and the Korean Studies Promotion Service of the Academy of Korean Studies (AKS-2019-KCL-1230004)

For the translation of *Ch'ŏngguyŏngŏn* (*Songs of the Green Hills*), we used the original *Ch'ŏngguyŏngŏn* assembled by The National Hangeul Museum as the basic text.

# Contents

*Acknowledgements* / v
*Introduction* / ix

Songs of the Green Hills: An Anthology of
    Korean Sijos / 001

    Preface / 002
    Sijos 1 – 580 / 005
    Postscript / 187

Glossary / 189
About the Translators / 194

# Introduction

Sijo is the oldest and best-known form of Korean poetry. In a tradition that includes hyangga,[1] Koryŏ dynasty folk songs, kyŏnggi-style poems, prose poems (kasa), and miscellaneous songs, sijo has been regarded as the most refined poetic form, comparable to Chinese quatrains and regulated verse or Japanese haiku, since its emergence in the 14$^{th}$ century, at the end of the Koryŏ dynasty—though questions remain about the exact date of its appearance.

Formally speaking, a sijo is an unrhymed poem of three lines, each of which has four segments or, in some cases, feet (音步). The length of each segment is the same; two segments make one phrase. Sijo, then, is a verse form with three lines of six phrases, which have four metrical segments. The first and middle lines have four segments of four syllables apiece, but the last line has some variations: the first segment of the last line must have three syllables, the second segment should have more syllables than expected, and the last line's cadence is thus called modified four segments. A sijo develops ideas through the rhythmic repetition of words in the first and second lines; rhythmic variation in the last line is how these ideas are completed. This rhythmic structure of repetition and variation is a defining aesthetic feature of a sijo. The last line usually ends with an exclamatory verb like hanora or an expressive verb like harira,[2] which highlights the speaker's

---

[1] Poems written using Chinese characters in a system known as hyangchal during the Unified Silla and early Goryeo periods of Korean history.
[2] Hanora means "I think so" or "I agree" and harira, "I will do so."

emotion and brings the section to a close.

The composition of sijos with three lines is thought to have inherited the structural characteristics of the three-paragraph composition of ten-line hyangga—a highly refined form, which generally has a three-part structure of 4-4-2 lines. Some exclamatory or expressive word begins the last line of a sijo—another legacy of the ten-line hyangga, which closes with an exclamation. Thus sijos have occupied a central place in Korean poetry since hyangga and continue to be practiced under the name of "the modern sijo."

A sijo with three lines and six phrases is called a common sijo (p'yŏngsijo), a single work is called a single sijo (tansijo), and a work consisting of several common sijos is called a serial sijo (yŏnsijo). Serial sijos are composed to express content that cannot be contained in a single common sijo; notable examples include T'oegye Yi Hwang's "Twelve Songs about Tosan" and Yulgok Yi I's "Nine Songs of Mountain Ko." Although there are excellent serial sijos, the form developed mainly through single sijos. The gentry, who produced and enjoyed sijo, also admired the kasa, a form of Korean lyric which can go on endlessly in its four-phrase composition. They composed long poems in Chinese characters, and so they did not feel much need to compose serial sijo. Nor was it unsuitable for them to sing their poems, since sijo was originally a poetic form intended to be sung.

Meanwhile, the long narrative sijo (sasŏl sijo) is a sijo longer than three lines and six phrases. The second line is usually prolonged, which suggests that the long narrative sijo has its own peculiar aesthetics beyond being merely an elongated variation of sijo. Unlike the upright and simple style of common sijo, a long narrative sijo embodies the aesthetics of deviation through a rhetoric of exaggeration and cataloguing. It deconstructs serious material by employing the exaggerated language of caricature. The three-line structure is retained regardless of the length of the poem. This distinguishes long narrative sijos from kasas, which can go on for several thousand lines without limitation through the repetitive use of four phrases.

Males from the gentry typically wrote sijos, which intellectuals from the nobility enjoyed. But even kings wrote sijos, and gisaengs enjoyed them, thanks to their special social status. In the late Chosŏn dynasty, the literary class expanded to include middle-class poets, who wrote sijos. For poetry written in Chinese characters, commoner poets formed poetry groups, while middle-class singer-poets organized singing groups, all to write sijos.

The singer-poets collected and published anthologies of sijos, fearing that the songs handed down by word of mouth would disappear unless they were printed. There are about 170 anthologies of sijos, the earliest of which was *Ch'ŏngguyŏngŏn (Songs of the Green Hills)* compiled by Kim Ch'ŏnt'aek in 1728. Here "Ch'ŏnggu (Green Hills) refers to Korea and "yŏngŏn" (elongating syllables) was a term for Korean song (sijo) at that time. Kim collected songs that were passed down or scattered in the works of individual writers, then edited and published them as *Songs of the Green Hills*, which has an important place in Korean literature, laying a solid foundation for the transmission of sijos by compiling the lyrics of sijo passed down in fragments. Along with *Popular Songs of the East (Haedongkayo*, 1755) edited by Kim Sujang and *Anthology of Korean Poetry (Kagokwŏllyu*, 1876) edited by Pak Hyogwan and An Minyŏng, this book is regarded as one of the three best anthologies of Korean sijos.

Let's consider the characteristics of *Songs of the Green Hills*. Kim's other name was Paekham or Isuk, his penname was Namp'a, and it is recorded that he worked as a p'okyo, an officer in the capital police, which we may assume he did for a short time when he was young. Little else is known about him, including the dates of his birth and death. He was probably born in the late 1680s, because he is placed just before Kim Sujang, who was born in 1690, on the list of ancient and modern singers in *Popular Songs of the East,* where fifty-six singers appear in the order of their age. Thus Kim must have compiled this book when he was in his forties.

Completing *Songs of the Green Hills* was no small task. Kim collected the lyrics, then proofread and corrected them, and then asked a middle-class acquaintance, Ch'angnae Chŏng, to write an introduction and a nobleman, Maaknoch'o Chŏngsŏp Yi, to write a postscript. It is thought he worked for more than ten years to finish the book.

*Songs of the Green Hills* contains 580 sijos, classified according to the tune, the writer, or the theme, the tune being the most widely used. From these three methods Kim produced a structural unity. Though it was the first anthology of Korean sijos, it was not merely a collection of lyrics but a refined anthology—which is why it is so highly valued in academia.

*Songs of the Green Hills* assigns the lyrics according to their tune to the chungdaeyŏp, saktaeyŏp, naksijo, and manhoengch'ŏngnyu groups. Chunhgdaeyŏp and saktaeyŏp belong to the daeyŏp tune, which is divided according to speed into the mandaeyŏp (slowest), the chunhgdaeyŏp (mid-speed), and the saktaeyŏp (fastest). The popular tunes were, in order, the mandaeyŏp, chunhgdaeyŏp, and saktaeyŏp until the 16th century, when the mandaeyŏp began to disappear, which is why there are no mandaeyŏp songs in *Songs of the Green Hills*. Chunhgdaeyŏp was the most popular tune in the 17th century, but it lost its popularity gradually at the beginning of the 18th century, and saktaeyŏp, which appeared in the latter 17th century, became the most popular tune in the late 18th century. This explains why there are only three songs in the chunhgdaeyŏp tune in *Songs of the Green Hills*.

Now let us examine how Kim classified songs according to the tunes in *Songs of the Green Hills*. Songs 1-3 are in the chunhgdaeyŏp tune. Among them, song 1 is ch'ojungdaeyŏp, song 2 is yijungdaeyŏp, and song 3 is samjungdaeyŏp. Song 4 is classified as pukjŏn and song 5, yipukjŏn. Songs 6-452 are in the saktaeyŏp group, with song 6 in the ch'osaktaeyŏp (the first tune of saktaeyŏp). But there is no mention of yisaktaeyŏp (the second tune of the saktaeyŏp) and songs 398-452 are in the samsaktaeyŏp (the third tune of saktaeyŏp). Thus the songs in between, 7-197, are in the yisaktaeyŏp. Accordingly, there are 391 lyrics in the yisaktaeyŏp tune, the most popular tune of that era.

Songs 453-462 fall under the heading of naksijo. Then comes song 463, "Changjinjusa: A Song to Offer Wine," and song 464, "Song of Meng Changjun." "Changjinjusa" is the name of the tune and title of Songang Chŏng Ch'ŏl's song to offer wine. The anonymous "Song of Meng Changjun" is the title of the song as well as its tune. These two songs were so popular they were added to *Songs of the Green Hills*. Lastly, the lyrics of songs 465-580 fall under the heading of manhoengch'ŏngnyu, long narrative sijos being separately collected here. The lyrics of these sijos appear to haves sparked some controversy, but Kim justifies their inclusion by arguing, "the lyrics of Manhoengch'ŏngnyu are obscene and trivial and cannot serve as a model to follow. But because they have a long history, they cannot be discarded all at once." And he includes a postscript by Maaknoch'o Yi Chŏngsŏp. The addition of 116 songs in the manhoengch'ŏngnyu tune enabled Kim to complete the geography of Korean songs as well as their division according to their tunes.

The songs in *Songs of the Green Hills* are also classified by authorship. The lyrics to songs 7-397 are in the yisaktaeyŏp tune, and Kim divided these songs into two groups: songs whose authors are known, and songs by anonymous writers.

The first group was arranged according to the writer's birth and death dates and social class. Works from the end of the Koryŏ dynasty fall under the heading of "the late Koryŏ dynasty": Song 7 by Mugŭn Yi Saek, song 8 by P'oŭn Chŏng Mongju, and songs 9-12 by Tongp'o Maengsasŏng. Then come songs by Chŏljae Kim Chongsŏ under "our royal court," e.g., the Chosŏn dynasty. King's songs appear separately under "Works by Kings": song 216 by King T'aejong, songs 217-219 by Hyojong, and song 220 by Sukchong. The works of six middle-class singer-poets are termed "Six Commoner Poets": Song 221 by Chang Hyŏn, 222-231 by Chu Ŭisik, 232-237 by Kim Samhyŏn, 238-245 by Ŏŭn Kim Sŏnggi, 246-255 by Kim Yugi, and 256-285 by Mamp'a Kim Ch'ŏnt'aek himself. Gisaeng songs are called "Three Ladies": 286-288 by Hwang Chini, 289 by So Paekchu, and 290 by Maehwa. The works of noble writers whose birth and death date is unknown fall under "Writers Whose Dates Are Unknown": 291 by Yim Chin, 292 by Yi Chungjip, and 293 by Sŏhojuin Yi Ch'ong.

Kim arranged the anonymous works in the yisaktaeyŏp tune group according to themes of his own devising, dividing them into 50 semi-units including poems of longing for the king, of rebuke and being sent into exile, of repaying a kindness, of rivers and lakes, of forests and leisure, poems about pleasures in the field and seclusion, of farm life, of knowing one's place. Some themes are similar but it is noteworthy how carefully Kim classified the lyrics.

In addition to the 580 songs, prose writings about some songs are recorded in *Songs of the Green Hills*. Thus after Nongam Yi Hyŏnbo's "Songs of a Fisherman" 18-22, Yi's reflections on the poems and T'oekye Yi Hwang's critical essay. Yi Hwang's serial sijo, "Twelve Pieces of Tosan" 27-38, is followed by Yi's essay on the sijo, "On 'Twelve Pieces of Tosan.'" Chŏng Ch'ŏl's sijos 39-88 are followed by Yi Sŏn's critical essay on them.

Songs of the Green Hills, the first anthology of Korean sijos, was systematically organized and relatively complete—which is why it exerted a great influence on the publication of subsequent sijo anthologies. Its title, Ch'ŏngguyŏngŏn, has become a common noun for a sijo anthology, and it has served as a model for many anthologies using the same title but have different systems of classification.

Songs of the Green Hills was published in manuscript form on May 16, 1728, but the existence of the original book cannot be confirmed. It was said the poet Oh Changhwan owned it, but when he went to North Korea, his father-in-law asked Lee Kyŏmno, the owner of T'ongmunkwan, a bookstore specializing in old books, to take care of Oh's books—which is how he came into possession of Songs of the Green Hills. Ch'ŏngguyŏngŏn: A Rare Book, published by the Chosŏn Rare Book Publication Company, has been the main reference. Some typos occurred in this edition, which were not easily corrected, since few had seen the original.

The National Hangeul Museum assembled the original Ch'ŏngguyŏngŏn in 2013, then hosted a special exhibit for the general public and a conference. A facsimile edition and an annotated edition of Ch'ŏngguyŏngŏn, edited by Kim Ch'ŏnt'aek, were published, making it possible for the general public to finally read the first anthology of Korean sijos. I hope Songs of the Green Hills, an invaluable Hangeul cultural resource, will provide a picture of Korea and its sijos in the late Chosŏn period for a long time to come.


In Sook Jeong
Professor
Department of Korean Literature and Linguistics
Sungkyunkwan University

# Songs of the Green Hills: An Anthology of Korean Sijos

# Preface

Poetry was integral to the songs of the ancients. When a song was expressed in letters, it became a poem. When a poem was played on a wind or a string instrument, it became a song. This is because song and poetry were once the same. The three hundred poems in *The Book of Poetry* spurred the development of ancient poetry, which in turn inspired modern poetry. Since then, however, song and poetry have divided in two. Rhyming poems have been called akpu[3] since the Han and Wei dynasties, but they were not popular among country people across the nation. There were also lyrics, another form of poetry known to the world since Qin and Sui dynasties, which were not as popular as poetry.

Producing lyrics is impossible unless one is not only good at writing but skilled in rhythms. Thus a good writer may not sing well and vice versa. There was no shortage of talent in our Royal Court, but few wrote lyrics, and even these were not handed down for long, because our nation values only literature, not music.

Namp'a Kim Paekham[4] is well-known in our nation for his singing and skillful use of rhythm. He studied literature, wrote lyrics for common people to learn, and collected the works of famous ministers and scholars and several hundred rhythmical songs of commoners. These he corrected and compiled into a book, for which he asked me to write a preface so that it might reach more people—a truly sincere idea. I took

---

[3] 樂府: Yuefu are Chinese poems composed in the style of folk songs; literally, "Music Bureau," a reference to the imperial Chinese government office charged with collecting or writing lyrics.

[4] Kim Ch'ŏnt'aek's other name. Namp'a was his penname.

it home and found the lyrics beautiful and charming. As to the meaning of the lyrics, some are peaceful and joyous, some are sad and painful, some are deep and lead, indirectly, to enlightenment. Some rise abruptly to soar and move the mind enough for readers to experience in advance signs of the prosperity and decline of the age, as well as the beauty and wretchedness of its customs. Lyrics and poetry go hand in hand, like ins and outs, and are indispensable to each other.

Ah, these lyrics were written not just to express ideas and evoke melancholy. There is something in them that lets people see and feel; hence putting them in a popular ballad would help edify people. Those lyrics are not as refined as poetry, though they possess many good and moral things, but why do the wise men of the world not collect them? Is it because only a few have a grasp of rhythm and so neglect them?

After several hundred years, P'aekham collected them to introduce to the people and hand them down to future generations. If writers know this fact in the nether world, they will say that P'aekham is surely Ziyun,[5] who appreciates them. He was already good at singing and wrote sinsŏng.[6] Kim made Ayangjigye[7] with geomungo master Chŏn,[8] and they trusted each other. When Chon played kŏmun'go and Kim sang the tune, the sound was so clear and bright it moved ghosts and radiated. Their skills were truly exquisite.

---

[5] 子雲: Penname of Yang Xiong, 揚雄, a Chinese poet, philosopher, and politician of the Han dynasty known for his philosophical writings and fu poetry compositions. Metaphorically, Ziyun is the man one waits for a thousand years to be appreciated.

[6] Literally, "new voice," referring to saktaeyŏp 數大葉 a popular 18th-century tune.

[7] 峨洋之契: Meeting of two masters, like the high mountain peak and the vast sea.

[8] Refers to Chŏn Manje, a master of kŏmun'go as well as of pip'a, a five-string mandolin.

I had suffered depression earlier and couldn't find anything to soothe my mind. Then P'aekham came with master Chŏn to sing lyrics, and my heavy heart softened.

Hŭgwa[9] wrote this preface in early March 1728.

---

[9] 黑窩: Penname of Chŏng Raegyo (鄭來僑, 1681-1759), a commoner Chŏson dynasty poet. His other penname was Wanam, and he was the author of *The Collected Works of Wanam*.

**Sijos 1-580**

**Ch'ojungdaeyŏp** 初中大葉: The first chungdaeyŏp[10] tune, the representative music of the 17th century, which in the next century was regarded as a slow tune.

1.

Let today be a day like this and every day be like today.
May it never end or begin again.
If it does begin again, let it be always like today.

**Ijungdaeyŏp** 二中大葉: The second chungdaeyŏp tune, the representative music of the 17th century, which in the next century was regarded as a slow tune.

2.

Look, people of Chu, where has your king[11] gone?
And his lands, six square li of lands—who owns them now?
Wuguan[12] is closed, and we don't have any news either.

**Samjungdaeyŏp** 三中大葉: The third chungdaeyŏp tune, the representative music of the 17th century, which in the next century was regarded as a slow tune.

3.

---

[10] Literally, the first moderately big piece.
[11] 楚義帝: Emperor Yi of Chu, the ruler of the Chu state in the late Qin dynasty. He was killed by Xiang Yu 項羽.
[12] 武關: one of four strategic mountain passes along the southern border of the Qin.

Feeble and unreliable is the supreme ruler of Western Chu!¹³
What does it matter if he conquered the whole country or not?
To whom will he leave his woman of unrivaled beauty and his
   swift horse?


**Pukchŏn** 北殿: Song music dating from the Koryŏ dynasty. Most *Scores for Zither Music,* including *Scores of Kŏmun'go,* are composed of three movements, while the songs have five.

4.

If you, lying alone, miss me, let's lie down together and roll.
It's all because of you, my love.
Let's get together and play, like thorns in coarse cotton wool.


**Ibukchŏn** 二北殿: A variation of pukjŏn. *Han'gŭmsinbo (New Scores for Korean Zither)* notes that it is composed of three movements, while the songs have five.

5.

Whoops, I dipped my weasel hairbrush in ink then dropped it
   outside the window.
Perhaps I can find it, when I go around.
Anyone who finds it will know its worth when he draws with
   it.

---

¹³ 項羽: Xiang Yu: The Ba Wang or Hegemon King of Western Chu during the Chu–Han contention period of China. A nobleman of Xiaxiang, Xiang Yu rebelled against the Qin dynasty and became a prominent warlord. He killed himself on the bank of the Wu River.

**Ch'osaktaeyŏp** 初數大葉: The first tune of saktaeyŏp, a representative 18th-century tune. The saktaeyŏp tune is faster than the chungdaeyŏp tune.

6.

Oh dear, my mistake, didn't I know I would miss her?
She wouldn't leave me when I urged her to stay. But after deliberately
Letting her go, I don't understand why I still miss her.

**Isaktaeyŏp** 二數大葉: The second tune of the saktaeyŏp, the representative 18th-century tune. The saktaeyŏp tune is faster than the chungdaeyŏp tune.

**The Late Koryŏ Dynasty**

**Yi Saek** (1328-1396): His penname was Mugŭn, and his other name was Yŏngsuk. He passed the state examination of the Yuan dynasty and worked as a drafter in the Hallim Academy. He was the chancellor during the reign of King Kongmin. He was best at writing and Confucian studies of his age. He was named Hansanbaek in our dynasty (the Chosŏn dynasty).

7.

Fierce clouds above the valley thick with snow.
Where did the plum tree open its pleasing blossoms?
Standing alone at twilight, I wonder where to drag my feet.

**Chŏng Mongju** (1377-1392): His penname was P'oŭn and his

other name was Talha. He was a chancellor during the reign of King Kongyang. When the fate of Koryŏ comes to an end, his body was gone along with his country. He was conferred Chief State Councilor posthumously in our dynasty, and Munch'ung is his posthumous title. He abolished the barbarian costume and followed Chinese custom, thereby boosting academic spirit.

8.[14]

If this body dies and dies again, even a hundred times,
And my bleached bones turn to dust, and my soul survives or not,
My unchanging red heart turning toward my Lord will never change.

**Maeng Sasŏng** (1360-1438): His penname was Tongp'o and his other name was Sŏngji. He won first place in the state exam in the Koryŏ dynasty and was Second State Councilor in our dynasty. His posthumous title is Munjŏng. Renowned for his filial piety, upright and frugal. He was also good at playing pipes and could handle three and four sounds as he wishes.

9.[15]

---

[14] Chŏng Mongju's answer to Yi Pangwŏn's (future King T'aejong) sijo 216. Before the Koryŏ dynasty ended, Yi asked Chŏng to help him establish the Chosŏn dynasty, singing sijo 216 (commonly called "Hayŏga, Song of What Matters"). Chŏng composed this sijo (commonly called "Tansimga, Song of the Red Heart") to express his loyalty to the Koryŏ dynasty.

[15] The first of four serial sijos called "Sasiga, Song of the Four Seasons in Nature." Sasiga is a series of songs sung to commemorate the four seasons. Maeng uses this poetic device to express his deep

Spring came to the rivers and lakes, a wild excitement rising naturally.
Makkŏlli[16] and mandarin fish served as side dishes by the stream.
I owe my life of leisure to the grace of the king.

10.

Summer has settled in the rivers and lakes. No work in the thatched house.
The trustworthy river raises a ripple to stir the wind.
I owe my cool summer days to my king's benevolence.

11.

Autumn has settled in the rivers and lakes, every fish has grown fat.
Loading a net in a small boat and spreading it out to float,
I spend my time leisurely, thanks to my king's benevolence.

12.

Winter has settled in the rivers and lakes, with more than one cha of snow.
Obliquely wearing a conical bamboo hat and putting on a straw raincoat,
I spent my days warm, all due to my king's benevolence.

---

gratitude to the king.
[16] Unstrained rice wine.

## Our Royal Court[17]

Kim Chongsŏ (1390-1453): His penname was Chŏljae and his other name was Kukkyŏng. He passed the state exam during the reign of King T'aejong and was Chief State Councilor. He was a man of great fidelity and resourcefulness. He was called a tiger, though he was of a small frame. He was assassinated in the Kyeyu Rebellion.

13.

The north wind blows through the top of a tree, the bright moon cold in the snow.
With a long sword in my hand, I stand guard at a ten thousand li distant border.
The sounds of my long whistle and loud shout—nothing stops me.

14.

We raised a flag on Mt. Changpaek and washed our horses in the Tuman River.
You petty, hard-boiled scholars! Aren't we also men of courage?
Look, who will be the first one enshrined at Kirin'gak?[18]

**Sŏng Sammun** (1418-1456): His penname was Maejuktang, his other name was Kŭnpo. He passed the state exam during the reign of King Sejong, became the member of the Reading Hall, and passed the higher civil office exam. He rose through

---

[17] The phrase means the Chosŏn dynasty.
[18] Kirin Shrine: A shrine in which portraits of meritorious subjects are exhibited.

the ranks to become the Royal Secretary-transmitter. He attempted to restore Prince Nosan along with Yi Kae (1417-1456). But his plan was uncovered and he was killed. Later, he was enshrined at Yuksin Shrine.

15.

Looking at Mt. Shouyang, I reproach Boyi and Shu Qi.[19]
Even if you were dying of hunger, how could you gather ferns?
Though it's only a plant, on whose land has it grown?

16.[20]

What will become of my body after I die?
Growing into a tall exuberant pine on the highest peak of Mt. Penglai,[21]
I alone will be green when white snow fills the earth and sky.


**Wang Pangyŏn** (Unknown): Director of the State Tribunal under King Sejong. He escorted Prince Nosan (to Yŏngwŏl); returning to Seoul, he wrote this sijo by a stream to express his feeling. We can find his love for the king in this single piece of song.

---

[19] 伯夷 Boyi and 叔齊 Shu Qi were the two princes of Guzhu in the Shang dynasty. They opposed King Wu's expedition against King Zhou of Shang and retreated to Shouyang Mountain, where they lived on fiddlehead ferns and eventually died of hunger.

[20] One of the so-called "Six Martyred Ministers." Sŏng Sammun tried to restore King Tanjong to the throne he had lost to Grand Prince Suyang (the future King Sejo). But the scheme was uncovered, and he was executed. This sijo expresses his undying loyalty to King Tanjong.

[21] 蓬萊山: a legendary land in Chinese mythology.

17.

Leaving my beloved king ten million li in the distance,
I sit by a stream, finding no place to rest my heart.
The water cries, like my heart, and flows along the night road.

## Songs of a Fisherman[22]

**Yi Hyŏnbo** (1467-1555): His penname was Nongam and his other name was Pijung. He passed the state exam during the reign of King Yŏnsan. He was a supervisor of the Central Council.

18.

Among many ways to live, a fisherman's life is carefree.
Floating in a tiny boat on the ten thousand ripples of the wide
    blue sea,
He forgets the human world. How can he tell how many days
    have passed?

19.

Look down: a thousand kil[23] of blue water. Look around:
    layers of blue mountains.
How much of the dust of the world, ten chang[24] long, covered
    them?
When the moon shines on the rivers and lakes, my mind

---

[22] Here "fisherman" is someone who has retired to nature to enjoy rural life and fishing, while waiting for a time to fulfill his ideal.
[23] A traditional unit of length. One kil is about 2.4 - 3 meters.
[24] A traditional unit of length. One chang is about 3 meters.

empties.

20.

I wrap steamed rice in a green lotus leaf, skewer fish with a willow branch,
And moor my boat among the reeds and heaps of silver grass.
I wonder who will know this pure clean taste.

21.

A leisurely cloud rises over the mountaintop and a white gull flies beside the stream.
These two are affectionate, thoughtless.
I'd like to forget my anxiety and follow you for the rest of my life.

22.

When I look around Changan,[25] the palace takes up a thousand li.
Even lying in a fishing boat, I have no time to forget.
Alas, it's not my worry. There should be a wise man who can save the world.


The author of the above two fisherman poems is unknown. When I grew old and retired from public service, I had nothing to do, so I gathered several pieces suitable for singing from among the poems the ancients recited, while holding a glass. I

---

[25] 長安 Changan, the ancient capital of more than ten Chinese dynasties, now known as Xi'an, is the name used for a capital or a large city.

taught them to male and female servants, and I censored them. I passed time, occasionally listening to them. Later, my boys found the songs and showed them to me. The lyrics were quiet, profound, and when people recited them they were liberated from rank and fame and sailed buoyantly away from the dust of the world.

These songs led me to throw away the lyrics I had enjoyed before and write them down with my own hands. I invited friends in the flower-blooming mornings and moon-rising evenings and let my maid sing on a small boat floating on the Pun'gang River.[26] It was hilarious, it made me forget my weariness. But there are many places where the words make no sense and are repeated: mistakes surely made in transcription. Because they are not sentences based on the teachings of sages, I adapted them haphazardly. I removed three out of twelve parts in the first song and made nine long lyrics to recite. I reduced the ten parts in the other song to five and sang them as yŏp.[27] These two songs became part of the new tunes.

While adding and deleting words according to the original meaning of the work, I cut a lot out, revised and added words, then titled it *Nongam's Unofficial Records*. I hope readers will not accuse me of seeking to rise above my place.

On the third day after Yudu,[28] 1549, Sŏlbinŏong,[29] the owner of Nongam, wrote this while traveling by boat on the Pun'gang River.

---

[26] Refers to the Naktong River running by Nongam's house in Tosan, Andong, Kyŏngsangbuk-do.
[27] A tune in which people sing different lyrics at that same time.
[28] The fifteenth day of June on the lunar calendar.
[29] Literally, an old fisherman with gray sideburns.

An old man made "Song of a Fisherman" from the songs he collected describing the life of a fisherman and stitched them together by inserting vernacular prose between them to create a long poem in twelve parts. The author's given name and family name are unknown. Once upon a time an old gisaeng in Andong Prefecture sang this song well. My uncle Songjae[30] invited her to sing it at a birthday feast for an old man. Young as I was then, I liked the song and wrote down its outline. I regret not recording the whole song.

Time passed, the song grew vague in my memory, and I fell into the dusty world, ever farther from the delights of nature. I wished I could hear the song for my own pleasure and to allay my worries. Whenever I went to the lotus pavilion in Seoul, I asked about it, but no old instrumentalists or singing gisaengs knew it. Thus only a few could enjoy this song.

A man named Pak Chun, who lived in Miryang, was famous for his knowledge of popular music. He gathered all the music of Chosŏn, classical court music and vernacular songs, and compiled them in a book, including this song and "Ssanghwajŏm."[31] But when people heard the songs, why did some lead them to dance in joy while others made them nod off? Because no one except Pak Chun knew them. How, then, can common people know this music?

Nongam, the honorable Sir Yi, left government service when he was over seventy and retired to the water-dividing bend to lead a life of leisure. Recalled several times, he refused to return. Wealth and fame he likened to floating clouds, and he cultivated a refined mellow taste beyond the

---

[30] Refers to Yi U (1469-1517): An official in the mid Chosŏn period. Myŏngjung was his other name, his penname was Songjae, Yi Hwang was his nephew, and he was Magistrate of Andong.
[31] A Koryŏ lyric composed during King Ch'ungryŏl's reign. The title means "The Dumpling Shop" or "The Turkish Bakery."

secular world. Rowing with a short oar in a small boat, he whistled at the dusk-covered river en route to the fishing rock. Befriending seagulls, he forgot worldly desires. He learned joy from watching fish jump. You could say he tasted real joy in nature.

Junior Secretary Hwang Chunggŏ[32] was a close friend of Sir Yi. He took the lyric of this song from Pak Chun's book and secured ten parts of the short poem, "Song of a Fisherman." He offered two to Sir Yi, who liked their simple elegance, but found their long phrases flawed. So he erased, corrected, and added to the lyrics, condensing twelve chapters into nine and the other ten parts into five. These he gave to the young servants for them to learn how to sing.

Whenever he met good friends or came across fine scenery, he would row them in a boat on the blue-mist-filled river, asking the children to sing in chorus, hold hands, and dance. Onlookers thought he was a hermit. Ah, he found true pleasure here, and of course he liked good songs. How to compare him to people who boost licentious thought while listening to the music of Zheng and Wei[33] and "Yushu Backyard Flower?"[34]

Sir Yi copied the book in his own hand and asked me to write a postscript. I'm like a draft horse, and my promise to the gulls has cooled. How can I talk about the joys of nature and fishing? I declined to do so many times, which did not dissuade him. Helpless, I wrote my impressions at the end of

---

[32] Refers to Hwang Chullyang (1517-1563). His other name was Chunggŏ, and his pennames were Kŭmgye and Nongam.

[33] 鄭衛 Zhengwei: Popular music in Zheng and Wei during the Warring States period. It refers to obscene songs and subversive music.

[34] 玉樹後庭花 Yushu Backyard Flower: An obscene song written by 後主 Houzhu of Chen, China, which helped lead to the fall of the Chen dynasty.

the book. As Su Shi[35] teased, it is no one else but I who says I want to retire to the mountains even as I maintain a lingering affection for the world.

On December 16, 1549, Yi Hwang, P'unggi Magistrate, bowed and wrote this humbly in his government office.

**Sŏ Kyŏngdŏk** (1489-1546): His penname was Hwadam, his courtesy name was Kagu. He worked as a civil servant during King Chungjong's reign. His posthumous title was Mun'gang.

23.

Fool that I am, everything I do is foolish.
No one will come to this secluded, deep mountain.
But with every falling leaf and rising wind I imagine it might
 be him.


**Song In** (1517-1584): His penname was Iam, and his other name was Myŏngjung. A son-in-law of King Chungjong, he was learned in the Great Learning and skilled in calligraphy. His posthumous title was Mundan.

24.

Buzzing around, hurrying everywhere,
What have I achieved? My days are almost over.
Alas, the past is gone. What can I do but play?

---

[35] Su Shi, courtesy name Zizhan, art name Dongpo, was a Chinese calligrapher, gastronome, painter, pharmacologist, poet, politician, and writer of the Song dynasty.

25.

I didn't put down the wine cup for thirty days in a month.
Nor did I suffer from either arm or mouth disease.
Why should I be sober if I don't get sick?

26.

I promptly forget what I hear and ignore what I see.
This is how I behave, so I don't judge how others behave.
I only hold my cup in my healthy hands.

**Yi Hwang** (1501-1571): His penname was T'oegye and his other name was Kyŏngho. He passed the civil service examination during Chungjong's reign and joined the Reading Hall. He was First Academician and Associate Councilor, becoming the head of Neo-Confucianism in the East. His posthumous title was Munsun.

**Six Pieces from Tosan**

27.

What does it matter if I do it this way or that?
What does it matter if a foolish country bumpkin is like that?
Why cure my chronic illness—enjoying nature?

28.

Making twilight my home, the wind and moon my friends,
I grow old along with this illness in this peaceful reign.
My only wish is not to find fault in this life.

29.

It is certainly not true that good customs have died,
That human nature is not virtuous.
Who tells such lies to delude the gifted people of the world?

30.

Mellow orchids in the valley: it's good to smell the fragrances of nature.
White clouds above the mountain: it's good to see nature.
Among these things, I miss that beautiful man[36] even more.

31.

A pavilion before the mountain and a stream below the pavilion.
A flock of gulls keeps on coming and going.
Ah, why does the pure white foal[37] have its mind set on a distant place?[38]

32.

Spring wind fills the mountain with flowers, autumn night fills the pavilion with moonlight.
The joy of the four seasons goes hand in hand with the joy of the people.
Fish leap and kites fly,[39] the shadow of a cloud and the light

---

[36] The king.
[37] A wise man rides a white foal. Here it means he lives apart from the king or as a recluse.
[38] The king lives far away.
[39] Refers to the mysterious order of nature.

of the sky[40] will never cease.

## Six More Pieces

33.

When I return from Ch'ŏllundae Pavilion, the Wallakche Study is clean.
My pleasure in living with ten thousand books is boundless.
But there is no greater pleasure than strolling.

34.

Though thunder splits the mountains, the deaf cannot hear.
Though the bright sun shines in the sky, the blind cannot see.
With clear eyes and ears, we must not be like them.

35.

The old men couldn't see me, nor I them.
Nevertheless their way lies before me.
How could I not follow them?

36.

You abandoned for all those years the way you once followed.
Where did you wander before you finally returned?
Now that you're here, don't think about anything else.

37.

---

[40] A metaphor for the harmonious state of the ten thousand things.

Why are green mountains always green?
And why do running waters never stop, day or night?
We, too, will never stop, we will stay green forever.

38.

How easy it is! Even the foolish know how to do it.
How hard it is! Even the wise cannot bring it to completion.
Easy or hard, we don't know how we're growing old.

"Twelve Pieces from Tosan" were written by an old man in Tosan.[41] Why did he write these songs? There are many obscene songs in our country, none deserving of mention. Though works like "Song of Confucian Scholars"[42] came from the mouths of literary men, they are arrogant and dissolute, also lewd and playful—not worth the respect of noblemen. Recently Yi Pyŏl's "Six Songs" became popular, and they say this one is better than another, but it only makes fun of the world, it's disrespectful, lacks generosity.

Though this old man had no knowledge of music, he knew he didn't like to listen to secular music. Chronically ill, in his free time he expressed his feelings in reading the poems that appealed to him. But these poems are different from the old ones; you can recite but can't sing them. To sing them, they must connect to our vernacular, the syllables of which force that on us.

Thus I wrote two earlier sets of "Six Pieces from

---

[41] Refers to T'oegye Yi Hwang himself.
[42] 翰林別曲 Hallim pyŏlgok: composed by young Confucian officials of the Academy of Letters during the period of military rule, a poem that vividly depicts the exulting view of life held by the literati now emerging onto the political stage.

Tosan" imitating Yi Pyŏl's "Six Songs." The first one expresses my will, the second, my knowledge. If you let children master them day and night, singing and listening to them, leaning on a cushion, and if you let them sing and dance by themselves, this may clean their mean hearts and allow them to progress. Then those who sing and those who listen will surely benefit. When I look back, my legacy is so different from the world, where these idle things may cause trouble. And I doubt these syllables will create harmony when set to music. For now I will make a copy and store it in a wooden box. I will often take it out to enjoy it and examine it myself, waiting for future readers to decide.

An old man in Tosan wrote this on March 16, 1565.

**Chŏng Ch'ŏl** (1537-1594) His penname was Songgang, and his other name was Kyeham. He won the first place in the national exam and joined the Reading Hall. His highest government post was Second State Councilor. He was Lord of Insŏng and his posthumous title was Munch'ŏng. King Sŏnjo said, "Even trees and grass know his steadfast loyalty and faithfulness. Among the many birds in the cabinet, he is a phoenix and a tiger in the palace."

39.[43]

My father begot me, and my mother raised me.
How could I live without the two of them?
I wonder where to repay their immense love.

40.

---

[43] This was the first of sixteen serial sijos titled "Songs of Illuminating People." He wrote these poems to illuminate people when he became the governor of Kangwŏn Province.

Brothers, touch your own bodies.
Who brought you into the world? Even your faces are the same.
You drank the same milk, so don't think differently.

41.

The king and his people are like the sky and the earth.
He wants to know my every sorrow.
How can I eat the fat water celery by myself?

42.

Serve your parents with all your heart and mind while they're alive.
When they're gone, your regret will be in vain.
This is perhaps the only thing you can't redo in your life.

43.

Dividing one body into two, he made a husband and a wife.
In life they grow old together, and in death they will go to the same place.
What silly people dare look askance at them?

44.

As men make a detour around the way that women take,
Women step off the road that men walk.
Unless they're your husband or wife, don't ask their name.

45.

What did your son learn from *The Book of Filial Duty*?
My son will finish *Lesser Learning* the day after tomorrow.

When will I see them finish both books and grow wise?

46.

My fellow villagers, let's do the right thing.
Born human, if we don't behave correctly,
How will we differ from cattle feeding, wearing a horsehair hat and cowl?

47.

If you hold my wrist, I'll hold you with both hands.
If you go out, I'll get your cane and follow you.
I'll take you home after the Hyangŭm ceremony.[44]

48.

No one is more trustworthy than a friend.
I can tell him all my thoughts.
How would I be better off without him?

49.

Ah, nephew, how can you live without food?
Ah, uncle, how can you live without clothes?
Please tell me about your hardship, I want to take care of you.

50.

How do you prepare the funeral service in your house?
When will your daughter be married off?

---

[44] An annual ceremony in October performed by Confucian scholars, who then drink together.

I'm not rich, but I want to make a donation.

51.

The sun is up. Let's go outside with our hoes.
After weeding my fields, we'll do yours.
On our way home, let's pick mulberry leaves to feed the silkworms.

52.

Although you have no clothes, don't steal them from others.
And though you're starving, don't beg others for food.
Once you smear yourself, the stains are hard to remove.

53.

Don't play ssangnyuk[45] or chess, or file a lawsuit.
Your house will fall, and you'll become an enemy of the people.
There are laws in this nation. Don't you know you're guilty?

54.

Old man carrying luggage on your head and back, please give it to me.
I'm young, even rocks aren't heavy for me.
Growing old is sad enough without having to carry this burden.

55.

People of Kangwŏn Province, don't sue your brothers.
Acquiring a slave or a patch of land isn't hard.

---

[45] A game of dice played at the beginning of the year and in winter.

But you give a sidelong scowl, wondering how to get more.

56.

After her husband's death, tears flow down her breasts.
Her child whines, says her milk is salty.
What heart can make that guy propose to her?

57.

When I rushed into Kwanghwamun Gate, at the Sangjikpang[46] in the Naepyŏngjo,[47]
Twenty gongs rang around the fifth watch[48] of the night.
This has become a thing of the past, a dream.

58.

The reverberating drum beat of the fifth watch on Mt. Penglai, where my beloved lies,
Travels over the clouds beyond the fortress and reaches the guest house window.
Whenever I come down to Kangnam,[49] I miss that sound.

59.

Bitter vegetables and warm water are better than meat.
A small thatched house means more to me.
Only what I feel for my beloved makes me anxious.

---

[46] Night duty room in the Naepyŏngjo
[47] An office in the Ministry of War.
[48] The sound of a gong tolling 4 a.m.
[49] South of the Han River. Here it refers to Ch'angp'yŏng, Chŏlla Province.

60.

When did Liuling⁵⁰ live? He was a wise man in the Jin dynasty.
Who is Kyeham?⁵¹ He's a hermit in our time.
Hold on. Why ask about a wise man and a hermit?

61.

Hey, man, how do you manage this household?
Pots are scarce and there are no small gourd bowls.
Who can you rely on when even offal and rice bran are not enough?

62.

If offal and bran are in short supply, and no gourd bowl can be found,
And even if he beggars this household,
I will live on believing in my beloved, if he loves me.

63.⁵²

What could I achieve, following you for ten years?
Are you saying you don't like me, that I'm wrong, do nothing?
What if I write a farewell letter and send you away?

64.

If I had wanted to achieve something, I wouldn't have clung to

---

⁵⁰ 劉伶 Liu Lian: One of the seven wise men in a bamboo forest during the Jin dynasty.
⁵¹ Refers to Chŏng Ch'ŏl himself. Kyeham is his other name.
⁵² The next three sijos are dialogues with wine.

you.
But I followed you, because you always greeted me cordially.
If you say I'm doing something wrong, I'll certainly quit.

65.

Listen to me once again: I can't live without you.
I have forgotten every difficulty, every bad thing, because of
   you.
How can I betray my old friend to love others?

66.

Even if you live to a hundred, isn't life fleeting?
What do I want to achieve in my ephemeral life,
Refusing to drink the cups others offer?

67.

If I flutter my wings two or three times here,
I could see my beloved on the first peak of Mt. Penglai.
What's the use of talking about something I can't do?

68.

If I break my body apart and let it float downstream,
The water will cry and flow into a ford on the Han River.
Only then may I be cured of the disease of loving my beloved.

69.

I'd like to cut up my heart to make the moon,
Hang it straight in the sky ninety thousand li away;
It will go on shining where my beloved lives.

70.

The cycle of rising and falling is endless. Taebangsŏng[53] is covered with fall grasses.
I'll play a reed to forget everything about the past
And drink a cup of wine in this peacefulness.

71.

When Sin Kunmang[54] worked as kyori[55] and I as such'an,[56]
We kept our guard duty outside Kŭnjŏngmun.[57]
The jade-like face of my beloved wavers before my eyes.

72.

Canopos[58] shines on Sigyŏngjŏng Pavilion.
Before the blue sea turns into a mulberry field and back again,
It produces new light as the days go by, it doesn't know when to fall.

73.

How long did the zelkova tree stand on the hill
Before a seed fell and a thin seedling grew old?
I will pour wine to celebrate its longevity.

---

[53] The old name of Namwŏn in Chŏlla Province.
[54] Sin Ŭngsi (1532-1585), who was Grand Censor. Kunmang was his other name.
[55] Fifth Councilor in the Office of Special Counselors, Academy of Talented Scholars, and Office of Diplomatic Correspondence.
[56] Fifth Councilor in the Office of Special Counselors.
[57] The Front Gate of Kŭnjŏngjŏn in the Kyŏngbokgung Palace.
[58] The brightest star in the constellation Carina and second brightest star in the sky.

74.

Crane flying high above a cloud in the blue sky,
Why did you come down? Do you like human beings?
It doesn't fly away until its long feathers fall to the ground.

75.

When I play taehyŏn[59] on the Korean zither, my heart melts.
I play a wu note[60] on the chahyŏn[61] and raise it to the mangmak note.[62]
I'm not at all sad, but what can I do with this farewell?

76.

I won't flap my wings again until my long feathers fall
And I fly high above the clouds in the blue sky.
I must see the unbounded, lovely world again.

77.

As the innkeeper of Sinwŏn,[63] I meet many customers.
They come and go and tell their different stories.
When I sit down to watch them, I see they're all working hard.

78.

---

[59] The third thick string of the six-string Korean zither.
[60] The highest note on the Korean pentatonic scale.
[61] The second thin string of the Korean zither.
[62] The highest among the seven notes of Korean music.
[63] The village name of Koyang, where the Chŏng Ch'ŏl's family burial ground and country house were located. It was called Sinwŏn, or new inn.

As the innkeeper of Sinwŏn, I wear a straw raincoat and bamboo hat.
Carrying my fishing pole in the fluttering drizzle, I keep going
To the water's edge, where the red-water pepper and white-water chestnut bloom.

79.

As the innkeeper of Sinwŏn, I closed the twig gate again
And made the flowing waters and green mountains my friends.
Boy, when a guest comes to Pyŏkche,⁶⁴ tell him I'm out.

80.

The thought of the King of Changsha,⁶⁵ Grand Mentor Jia,⁶⁶ makes me laugh.
He seemed to bear all the burdens of the people by himself.
A deep sigh and tears are more than enough. Why such bitter wailing?

81.

I know my features are no better than any others,
And I don't use powder, or wear eye makeup, or apply rouge,
And so I doubt if he will ever love me.

---

⁶⁴ Refers to Pyŏkche station, near Sinwŏn.
⁶⁵ 長沙 The history of Changsha, the capital of central China's Hunan province, dates back to the Zhou dynasty (1046–256 B.C.).
⁶⁶ 賈誼 Jia Yi, a Chinese poet and politician of the Western Han dynasty, is best known for writing the first fu rhapsodies. When he became Grand Mentor of Changsha, passing Xiang Shiu (湘水), he wrote *Lament for Qu Yuan* (吊屈原賦), who had drowned a century before, at Miluoshui (汨羅水), and cast it into the water.

82.

When the tree sickened, no one rested in the pavilion.
When it leafed out, every passerby rested under the tree.
After its leaves fell and its boughs were cut, no birds came.

83.

Tall, exuberant pine trees are felled, alas, felled.
If you leave them alone for a while, they will grow into good timber.
If the Hall of Rectitude sinks, what can we use to support it?

84.

After ten years, I see the white jade cup[67] of Chungsŏdang[68] again,
Pure white, the same as it was in the old days.
Why do people's minds change by day and night?

85.

Yesterday I heard that the rice wine at Kwŏnnong[69] Sŏng's[70] house was ready,
So I kicked a sleeping cow until it stood up and I spread a saddlecloth over it to ride.
Boy, is Kwŏnnong in the house? Tell him that Overseer Chŏng has arrived.

---

[67] A wine cup made of white jade bestowed by the king.
[68] Another name for the Office of Special Advisers.
[69] The board member of a community association.
[70] A reference to Sŏng Hon (1535-1598), a scholar and official in the mid-Chosŏn period. His penname was Ukye.

86.

Why do they use good timber this way?
There are too many plans for this tilting, demolished house.
Will the many carpenters, holding black ink pot and rulers, rush about in vain?

87.

Where would that boat rocking in the storm go?
It should not have sailed under these menacing clouds.
You must be careful if you have a flimsy boat.

88.

That pine tree over there stands next to the road.
I'd like to bring it in and dig a hole for it.
Anyone carrying a straw rope and axe might chop it down.


The poems above were written by Minister Songgang Chŏng Munch'ŏng.[71] His poetry and lyrics are not only clear and refreshing but also uniquely important because they often became a topic of conversation among the people. His skillful songs were praised in every age, his long and short poems are handed down everywhere. Even Qu Yuan,[72] Li Sao,[73] and Su

---

[71] Chŏng Ch'ŏl's posthumous title.
[72] 屈原 Qu Yuan was a Chinese poet and politician who lived during the Warring States period. He was known for his patriotism and contributions to classical poetry.
[73] 離騷 "Li Sao" is a Chinese poem from the anthology *Chuci*, which dates from the Warring States period of ancient China and is generally attributed to Qu Yuan.

Zizhan's[74] poems are hardly said to be better than his poems. When I listened to him singing with his high clear voice, I felt myself instantly free of my body, as though I were soaring on new wings into the sky to fly on the wind to the hermit's world. His love for the king and the patriotic zeal of his lyrics sadden people. They sigh and ask, who can compete with Chŏng, if his loyalty did not derive from Heaven or was even rarer?

Ah, Lord Chŏng, an honest upright man who lived at a time when factional discussions were rampant, slander and accusations widespread, and you could be convicted from on high by the king and envied from below by other court members. He lost his government position and was exiled. He was nearly put to death then spared. But the slander and rebukes were worse after his death. Su Zizhan's suffering was once said to be the most extreme, but his poems of longing for the king were read and enjoyed in the palace. But the king did not even know of Chŏng's poems of longing for him. How could his misfortune be so great?

Lord Ch'ŏngŭm Kim Munjŏng,[75] discussing the beginning and end of Lord Chŏng's life, rightly compared his loyalty to Qu Yuan's. His lyrics were published in the Northern Province in the old days. But to our great sorrow they were not handed down to us thanks to the passing of the years and the war we fought. I, a stupid person, was convicted in a peaceful time and exiled. Living far from the king and my parents, I couldn't find anyone to whom I could unburden myself.

---

[74] 子瞻 Zizhan, the courtesy name of Su Shi (art name, Dongpo), was a Chinese calligrapher, gastronome, painter, pharmacist, poet, politician, and writer in the Song dynasty.
[75] Refers to Kim Sanghŏn (1570-1652): An official in the mid Chosŏn period. His other name was Sukto, his penname was Ch'ŏngŭm, and he liked Chŏng Ch'ŏl's "Song of Longing for My Beloved" so much that he sang it with his servants.

Sauntering by the pond, I recited poems, taking only this one to correct its errors and copy it carefully. I kept it in my desk and read it aloud, which helped me forget my worries. This was to mimic, arrogantly, what Zu Xhi did to lighten his gloomy heart when he wrote *Collected Commentaries on the Songs of Ch'u*.[76]

Wansanhuin Yi Sŏn wrote this in early January 1690, in the Yuranhŏn Office, in Ch'asŏng.

**Pak Kyewŏn**: His other name was Kunok, and his penname was Kwanwŏn. He passed the civil service examination during King Myŏngjong's reign and was Minster of War.

89.

Dozens of friends sat down in Orye Fortress on a moonlit night.
Who would not weep at such homesickness?
I think I'm the only one whose heart is loyal to the nation.

**Yang Ŭngjŭng**: His other name was Kongsŏp, and his penname was Songch'ŏn. He passed the civil service examination during King Myŏngjong's reign and was chief magistrate.

90.

With a bowl of rice and a bottle of water in peacetime,
I wander lightly, letting my sleeves out.
Nothing hinders me in this world, and I like that.

---

[76] 楚辭集註: Notes from the Chu Ci Collection, *Collected Commentaries on the Songs of Ch'u*.

91.

Wearing a linen cloth in bitter cold, enduring rain and snow in the rock cave,
I have never even enjoyed the sunlight shining through the clouds
But I am moved to tears when I hear the sun has set in the western mountains.[77]

**Kim Hyŏnsŏng**: His other name was Yŏkyŏng, and his penname was Namch'ang. He passed the civil service examination during King Myŏngjong's reign and was chief magistrate of Tollyŏngbu Office. He was a good writer and calligrapher.

92.

What a happy day, and how happy it is!
I'm afraid this happy day will come to an end.
What do I care if every day is like today?

**Sŏ Ik**: His other name was Kunsu, and his penname was Manjuk. He passed the civil service examination during King Sŏnjo's reign and was the Ŭju magistrate.

93.

If I tear down this mountain and reclaim the sea,
I can travel by foot to see my beloved on Mt. Penglai.

---

[77] Refers to the death of King Chungjong.

I'm like a Jingwei,[78] all I do is wander around.

94.

Like an unbridled horse on green grass by a river after rain,
I raise my head and neigh toward the North.
I cry because I miss my Lord when the sun sets over the pass.

**Hong Chŏk**: His other name was Taeko, and his penname was Haŭja. He passed the civil service examination during King Sŏnjo's reign and was a member of the Reading Hall. His public service culminated in Sain.[79]

95.

Did snow also fall on Saje[80] yesterday?
Snowflakes look like sand, and sand like snowflakes.
The affairs of the world are, perhaps, just like this.

**Pak Illo** (1561–1643): A military official during King Sŏnjo's reign, who was a myriarch. Looking at the prematurely ripe persimmon on the table, Hanŭm[81] asked Pak Illo to write three sijos, expressing his yearning for his parents.

---

[78] 精衛, Jingwei: A legendary bird in ancient China. The original Emperor Yan's little girl drowned in the East China Sea and was reincarnated as a bird.

[79] 舍人 A drafting adviser in the Office of Special Councilors.

[80] Sand dunes on Monggŭmpo beach in Changyŏn-hyŏn, Hwanghae Province.

[81] Refers to Yi Hangpok, a literary man and politician in the middle period of Chosŏn. He was Junior Assistant Secretary and Chief State councilor

96.

The prematurely ripe persimmon on the small dining table looks beautiful.
It's not a Chinese lemon, but it's worth clutching to my breast.
The one who was supposed to greet me isn't here, which saddens me.

97.

Catching Wang Xiang's [82] carp, cutting Mang Zong's [83] bamboo shoot,
And wearing Lao Laizi's[84] cloth until my black hair turns gray,
I will perform my filial duty all my life, like Zengzi.[85]

98.

I will extract threads from ten thousand kyun,[86] braid them into a long cord,
And bind up the travelling sun in the ninety thousand li distant

---

[82] 王祥, Wang Xiang (184 – 268): A famous filial son in the Jin dynasty. When his stepmother wanted to eat carp one winter, he cracked the ice in a frozen river, and a carp leaped out.

[83] 孟宗, Meng Zong: A famous filial son of the Wu dynasty. When his mother wanted to eat bamboo shoot one winter, he went to the bamboo grove and wept. Legend has it that a bamboo shoot suddenly appeared before him.

[84] 老萊子, Lao Laizi (599 BC – 479 BC): A Chu man in the Spring and Autumn period famous for his devotion to his parents. There is a legend that he wore children's clothes and performed cute tricks to please his parents when he was seventy years old.

[85] 曾子: Refers to Zeng Shen(曾參), one of Confucius's disciples, famed for his filial duty.

[86] A traditional measure of weight. 1 kyun is 30 kŭn, about 1800 g.

sky—
Anything to keep my gray-haired parents in Puktang from growing older.

99.

A crow flew into a crowd of phoenixes.
It looks like a stone in a heap of white jade.
The phoenix also belongs to the family of birds—it won't be bad to play together.

What was this song written for? To express what my great-grandfather, Minister Hamŭm,[87] who died in the spring of 1611, thought of Myriarch[88] Pak Illo.[89] That generation was long gone, and the song was not handed down. I was afraid it would disappear in later generations, and secretly lamented its passing for a long time.

    This unworthy grandson Yunmun[90] was appointed Magistrate of Yŏngch'ŏn in the spring of 1690. Pak Illo came from this region, the song was handed down to the present, and his descendants are still alive. On a moonlit night, free from governmental affairs, I listened to his grandson Chinsŏn sing. All at once it seemed that latecomers were waiting for him

---

[87] Penname of Yi Tŏkhyŏng (1561-1613). He was First Academician, Third State Councilor, Second Stat Councilor, and Chief State Councilor.
[88] The fourth-ranked military officer at a naval base.
[89] 朴仁老 (1561~1642). He commanded ten thousand men at Chorap'o Port.
[90] Refers to Yi Yunmun (1646-1717), whose other name was Saong. Great-grandson of Yi Tŏghyŏng, he was Second Censor-Inspector, Magistrate of Yŏngch'ŏn, and Mayor of Imsil.

in the mountains and waters of Yongjin.⁹¹ Sadness overcame me, and I wept. So I had three long and four short songs engraved to spread them widely. I did this on March 3, 1690.

**Yi Tŏkhyŏng**: His other name was Myŏngpo, his penname was Hanŭm. He passed the civil service examination during King Sŏnjo's reign and was a member of the Reading Hall. He was First Academician and Chancellor of the National Academy at the same time. His final government post was Chief State Councilor, and his posthumous title was Munik. When Pongnae Yangsaŏn saw him at the age of fourteen, he was surprised and said, "He really deserves to become my teacher."

100.

Pouring wine into a big cup and drinking until I'm drunk,
I count heroes from the old days down to the present.
Liu Ling⁹² and Li Bai,⁹³ I assume, are my friends.

**Yi Hangbok**: He passed the civil service examination during King Sŏnjo's reign and was a member of the Reading Hall. He was Chief State Councilor. His other name was Chasang, his penname was Paeksa, and his posthumous title was Munch'ung.

---

⁹¹ The old name of Yangsuri where the North Han and South Han Rivers merge. Yi Tŏkhyŏng retired from government to spend the rest of his life here.
⁹² 劉伶 Liu Ling: One of the Seven Bamboo Sages, famed for his drinking abilities.
⁹³ 李白 Li Bai (701-762): A famous T'ang dynasty poet. It is said he drank three hundred cups a day and drowned, drunkenly trying to catch the moon reflected on the Cai Shihiang (彩石江).

101.

Our time is like this, and human affairs are like that.
When it's like this, how can it be otherwise?
People say this and that, and I can't help but sigh.

102.

Setting a date to return to the rivers and lakes, I've been busy for ten years.
My ignorant white dog complains that I am too slow.
My king's favor is extremely dear, and I'll return after I repay it.

103.

Oh, cloud that rests on the high peak above Ch'ŏllyŏng Pass,
How about setting afloat the resentful tear of a lonely vassal, like rain,
And scatter it over the nine-fold-deep palace, where my beloved is.

**Yi Chŏnggu**: His other name was Sŏngjing, his penname was Wŏlsa. He passed the civil service examination during King Sŏnjo's reign and was a First Academician and Chancellor of the National Academy at the same time. His final government post was Third State Councilor. His posthumous title was Munch'ung. His name was known worldwide for his memorial written in the year of musul.

104.

Can I believe my beloved? He is truly unbelievable.
I realize that even trustworthy time is unreliable.

Hard as it is to believe, what can I do but believe?

**Yu Chasin**: During King Sŏnjo's reign, he was the mayor of Seoul. He is Yu Hwibun's father.

105.

Autumn mountain at twilight sinks into the river.
I sit with my fishing pole in a small boat.
Heaven thinks I'm lonely and sends the moon to follow me.

**Nam I**: He was Minister of War during King Sŏnjo's reign.

106.

I draw a long sword and climb Mt. Paektu.
The bright world sinks into dust that smells of fish.
When can I shake off the dust fluttering from the North and
   South?

**Paek Ho**: His other name was Chasun, and his penname was Paekho. He passed the civil service examination during King Sŏnjo's reign and was a secretary in the Ministry of Rite.

107.

Are you lying down or sleeping in a valley covered with thick
   green grass?
Where did your rosy face go when the white skeleton was
   buried?
I'm sad I cannot offer this cup to anyone.

**Cho Ch'anhan**: His other name was Sŏnsul, and his penname was Hyŏnju. He passed the civil service examination during King Sŏnjo's reign and was a Royal Secretary. He was a good writer.

108.

I entered the house of a powerful family to sell off my poverty and lowliness.
But who wants to bargain when there is no premium?
I asked for rivers and mountains, wind and moon—he couldn't do that.

109.

Where do I rank, and who are the heroes?
Rising and falling through time is nothing but a dream in a dog's nap.
Why do these fools urge me not to enjoy myself?


**Hong Sŏbong**: His other name was Hwise, and his penname was Haggok. After passing the civil service examination during King Sŏnjo's reign, he was a member of the Reading Hall, rising to the rank of Chief State Councilor. He was designated Lord of Iksŏng.

110.

Did I or did I not shed tears and blood when we parted?
The flowing water of the Amnok River wears no blue at all.
The gray-haired boatman says he has never seen such a thing.

**Yi Sunsin** (1545-1598): He passed the national military examination during the reign of King Sŏnjo. He was Commander-in-Chief of the Naval Forces. His posthumous title was Ch'ungmu. As a man of wisdom and strategy, he built "Turtle Ships" during the Imjin War when he was Commander of Navy Forces of Chŏlla Province and defeated Japanese armies.

111.

When I sit alone in the moonlight, in a watch tower on Hansan Island,
Moored in anxiety, with a sword by my side,
A reed pipe playing somewhere carves up my bowels.


**Cho Chonsŏng**: His other name was Such'o, his penname was Yongho: He passed the civil service examination during King Sŏnjo's reign and was Second Minister in the Office of the Royal Clan. His posthumous title was Somin.

He wrote four of the so-called "Calling Boy Poems" and translated them into Chinese.

112.

Boy, where's your mesh bag? It's getting late in the western mountains.
The bracken has already grown stiff overnight.
How can I eat breakfast and dinner without this vegetable?

113.

Boy, prepare my straw raincoat and bamboo hat. Rain fell on

the eastern stream.
Tie a barbless hook on a long fishing pole.
Fish, don't be scared. I'm just here to enjoy myself.

114.

Boy, bring me porridge for breakfast. We have lots of work to do in the southern field.
Who will work this poor weeding plow with me?
Ah, plowing in peacetime is also due to the grace of the king.

115.

Boy, feed the ox to go to North Village and drink new rice wine.
The ox carries a drunken face under the moonlight.
Ah, today I saw a Sihuangshangren[94] again.

**Sin Hŭm** (1566–1628): His penname was Sangch'on and his other name was Kyŏngsuk. He passed the Civil Service Examination during the reign of King Sŏnjo and was promoted to Chief State Councilor during the King Injo's reign. His postmumous title was Munjŏng.

116.

Snow falls on a mountain village, burying the stone road.
Don't open the twig gate: no one will come to see me.
A sliver of the bright moon at midnight is my only friend.

117.

---

[94] 羲皇上人, pre-Fuxi people; a carefree person leading a life of leisure.

What's fame? An old discarded shoe.
I return to the country, where inermis and deer are my friends.
Living a hundred years like this is also due to the grace of the king.

118.

Why are only pine trees and bamboo green when the rest of the vegetation is buried?
Why are you alone green when wind and frost mix?
Stop asking questions. That is their nature.

119.

Were the Four White-Haired Ones[95] real? It was Liuhou's[96] superb tactic.
If they were in fact real, they would not come out.
But they became Lu Zhi's[97] guests, pretending otherwise.

120.

---

[95] 商山四皓: The Shangshan Four, also known as the Four White-Haired Ones because of their white eyebrows and hair, were Dongyuan Gong, Xia Huanggong, Yu Liji, and Yuli. To escape the chaos of the Qin dynasty, they lived in seclusion on Shangshan Mountain.

[96] 張良, Zhang Liang (courtesy name, Zifang), was a strategist and statesman of the early Western Han dynasty. He was one of the "Three Heroes of the early Han dynasty," along with Han Xin and Xiao He.

[97] 呂后, Empress Lu Zhi, commonly known as Empress Lü and formally as Empress Gao of Han, was the Empress Consort of Gaozu, the founding emperor of the Han dynasty.

Who are the Yangsaeng?[98] True scholars indeed.
They were unknown in the Qin dynasty and didn't appear in the Han dynasty.
Then why did Shusan Tong[99] ask if they had arrived or not?

121.

After the snow stopped falling last night, the moon began to shine.
Moonlight after snow is unbelievably bright.
But why does the cloud at the edge of the sky sail back and forth?

122.

Why does the black-crowned night heron stand by the stream?
What can it gain by watching for careless fish?
How about forgetting the fish, since you live in the same water?

123.

Whether rafters are long or short, and pillars tilted or twisted,
Don't scoff at the small thatched house with two rooms.
Ah, the moonlight pouring through the vines on the mountain is all mine.

124.

---

[98] Two virtuous scholars of the Lu dynasty who refused to serve the Han dynasty.
[99] 叔孫通, Shusun Tong was an official and ritual specialist who served in the Qin and Western Han courts. He organized the first court worship of Emperor Gaozu of Han and took custody of the young Crown Prince Ying, the future Emperor Hui.

Where did the two Queens[100] go after the sun set over Mt. Cangwu?[101]
What sorrow overcame them when they did not die at the same time?
Only the bamboo grove,[102] I suppose, knows that.

125.

Though I know it's wrong to drink and play,
Didn't you see the people plowing over Lord Xinling's[103] grave?
How can we not play, when a hundred years are transient?

126.

When I crossed Rou Shui[104] to meet the immortal hermit,
Jade Lady and Golden Boy[105] came out to ask,
"Where did Jupiter[106] go?" I think I'm it.

127.

That foolish roc bird is truly laughable!
Why did you soar into the ninety thousand li distant sky?

---

[100] Refers to Ehuang and Nuying, two queens of Emperor Shun.
[101] 蒼梧山, Cangwu Mountain, where Emperor Shun died.
[102] Two queens travelling to the Xiaoxiang River (瀟湘江) in search of Emperor Shun could go no farther because of the water. They shed bloody tears, which fell on the bamboo and turned into red dots.
[103] 信陵君, Lord Xinling, born Wei Wuji, was a prominent aristocrat, statesman, and general in the Warring States period and one of the Four Lords of the Warring States.
[104] 弱水, Ruo Shui is a major river system in northern China.
[105] A fairy man and woman living in a fairyland.
[106] An immortal hermit.

Korean crow-tits and sparrows are perfectly happy in the pit.

128.

Don't ask about me, I was Zhuxiashi[107] in my previous life.
How many years passed before I returned, after leaving on a blue cow?[108]
Having too many things to do in the world, I don't know if I returned or not.

129.

Once right and wrong disappear, glory and shame cease to matter.
After putting aside my geomungo and books, I'm free.
White seagull, only you and I have forgotten the things of the secular world.

130.

Rain fell in the morning, and wind blew later in the day.
What rain and wind are these on my ten thousand li road?
Well, resting is not a bad idea, since twilight is still far away.

131.

Drawing my beloved's features with blood scooped out of my heart,
I want to hang it on the white wall in the high house and gaze at it.

---

[107] 柱下史, Zhuxiashi. Because Laozi was the Keeper of the Archives in the Zhou dynasty, the word generally refers to him.
[108] 青牛: The cow Laozi rode when he traveled to the West.

Who invented separation as a way of killing people?

132.

Spring hues everywhere when rain falls on the night after Hansik.[109]
Even unfeeling flowers and willows bloom, knowing their time has come.
But why does my beloved never return after leaving me?

133.

Every pomegranate blossomed after last night's rain.
I draw the jade curtains by the lotus-blooming lake.
For whom am I so anxious? Why can't I find any relief?

134.

A rustling sound outside the window—I rise to see if it's my beloved.
What fallen leaves line the road where orchids grow?
Ah, I'm afraid my bowels and intestines may be torn apart.

135.

When the light burns bright in a silver lamp and incense fades in the burner,
I wake up and sit alone beside the deep lotus-patterned drapes.
I can't sleep with the noisy drumbeat of the night watch.

136.

---

[109] The Day of Cold Food, the 105th day after the winter solstice.

They say spring has come, but I can't feel the tide.
The green willow by the stream knew it before I did.
How can I deal with this separation from other people?

137.

Away from the human world, I feel free.
In a straw raincoat I climb to the fishing hole.
I laugh, wondering why Jiang Ziya[110] doesn't return.

138.

After cultivating two furrows in the deep valley of Mt. Nam,
I plant all the elixir of life I dug out of Mt. Sanshen.[111]
Only I will see how the blue sea turns into a mulberry field.

139.

How many different wines do you have? Clear wine and raw rice.
I only drink to get drunk; it doesn't matter if it's clear or raw.
Tonight the moon is bright, and the wind is clean: what does it matter if I don't sober up?

140.

Though a firefly becomes "fire," it's not "fire" but a firefly.
If a stone becomes a star, it's still a stone, not a star.

---

[110] 太公望, Jiang Ziya, who was known by several other names, was a Chinese nobleman who helped King Wen and Wu of Zhou overthrow the Shang in ancient China.
[111] 三神山: Where immortals live in the legends of the East China Sea.

I don't know if they are in fact "fire" and star.

141.

As flowers fall and new leaves sprout, the season changes.
A green bug in the grass becomes a butterfly and flies around.
Who plays this trick and makes ten million changes?

142.

I was born too late to know antiquity.
When people stopped using quipu, worldly affairs increased.
I'd rather enter the village of wine and forget the world.

143.

Wine in the jug and many guests in their seats.
How can I see that great man Kong Rong[112] again?
What's the use of talking about anybody else?

144.

The composer must have had many worries.
Unable to express them in words, did he empty them into songs?
If I can empty my worries, I will also sing.

145.

---

[112] 孔門舉, Kong Rong, courtesy name Wenju, was an official, scholar, and minor warlord in the late Eastern Han dynasty. A 20th-generation descendant of Confucius, he was once the Chancellor of Beihai State and was also known as Kong Beihai.

After pohŏja[113] ended, yŏmillak[114] followed.
The listeners' excitement increases in the wu and the kyemyŏn notes.[115]
Boys, don't play sangsŏng,[116] I'm afraid the sun will set.

The graceful and elegant[117] songs of China are recorded in books. But the so-called songs of our country are only used as entertainment when people host guests. They are neither regarded as poetry nor included in a book, because the sound of our vernacular is different. The Chinese speaking voice naturally turns into letters, but our speaking voice must be translated into Chinese to become letters. For this reason, though we have our share of writers, nothing is handed down as popular ballads or new music. It's deplorable.

    I retired to the countryside, because I was sick of the world, which had forsaken me. When I look back, the glory and fame of the past are useless as chaff, discarded grain, or composting grass. But when I came across something and sang it, I was like Feng Fu[118] who climbed from his carriage to catch

---

[113] 步虛子, Pacing the Void: Tang music introduced during the Koryŏ dynasty, which began as court and private instrumental music during the Chosŏn period.

[114] 與民樂, Enjoyment with the People: Music composed during King Sejong's reign. *Song of the Dragon Flying to Heaven* (龍飛御天歌) was sung to this music, which began as court and private instrumental music during the late Chosŏn period.

[115] Traditional Korean musical notes, wu being clear and gallant and keymyŏn, melancholy.

[116] 商聲, Shangsheng: A scale that depends on shang, one of the five notes in Chinese music; a sad tune.

[117] 風雅: Refers to the "Airs of the States" in *The Book of Odes*; also used to refer to poetry.

[118] 馮婦, Feng Fu: "Feng Fu was a man in Chin who was good at

a tiger. It was like a disease: I couldn't give up acting with reckless abandon. If anything moved me, I turned it into a poetic phrase; if it was unsatisfactory, I wrote a lyric in the vernacular to sing and recorded it in the Korean alphabet. Because this is only a song from a remote place about separation, it cannot be circulated in poetic circles. Though it was written for fun, there is something worthy in it to consider.
     Pang'ong wrote this on the winter solstice of 1613, in a farmhouse in Kŏmp'o.

**Kim Kwanguk**: His other name was Hoei, and his penname was Chukso. He passed the civil service examination during King Kwanghaegun's reign and was Minister of Justice and Deputy Director.

146.

After Tao Yuanming's[119] death another Yuanming appeared.
Pammaŭl's old name happens to be the same.[120]
My return to a humble life in the country is not different from

---

seizing tigers, but eventually became a good official. Many years later he went out into the country and found a crowd of people chasing a tiger. They cornered the tiger against some cliffs, but no one dared tangle with it. When they saw Feng Fu, they ran to greet him. And seeing him boldly roll up his sleeves and climb out of his carriage, they were delighted. But the other scholars there only laughed" (*Mencius*. David Hilton Trans. 186)

[119] 陶淵明, Tao Yuanming, also known as Tao Qian or Tao Ch'ien, was a Chinese poet who lived during the Eastern Jin and Liu Song dynasties, considered one of the greatest poets of the Six Dynasties period.

[120] The village of chestnuts becomes Yulli (栗里 Lili) in Chinese. Tao Yuanming also returned to Lili, Jiangxi Province. Pammaŭl is the village where Kim Kwanguk retired.

his.

147.

I have forgotten fame, riches, and honor.
I gave away and forgot all the cumbersome things of the world.
I forgot myself. How can others not forget me?

148.

From my neighbor I borrowed less than a mal of coarse barley,
Which I pounded and rubbed, brewed and filtered.
Whether it tastes sweet or bitter hardly matters to a starving mouth.

149.

This entirely quiet and beautiful landscape was given to me.
I'm its sole owner—who will dispute that?
Others may think I'm ill-tempered, but I won't share it.

150.

After washing the earthen pot and drawing water from the spring under the rock,
I cook sweet adzuki-bean gruel and take the salted kimchi from the crock,
Which are so delicious I don't want others to know what they taste like.

151.

Why, oh why, is that white gull working so hard?
It circles the field of reeds, looking for fish.

How about just mindlessly sleeping, like me?

152.

With nothing to do on a long sunny day, under the eaves of a thatched house,
I napped on a cattail mat until I woke at sunset.
Someone hemmed and hawed outside the door, asking me to go fishing.

153.

They say the three State Councilors[121] are precious; I wouldn't trade this landscape for them.
I load the moon on my boat and cast my fishing line here and there.
Pure joy! Why should I envy powerful, wealthy men?

154.

Under the bright moon on the autumn river I row my little boat alone.
When I cast my line, it startles the sleeping gulls.
The sound of a fisherman's pipe somewhere adds to my joy.

155.

I threw away all my dizzying, troublesome papers,
Whipped the horse, and returned in the autumn wind.
Even a bird freed from its cage would not feel so refreshed.

---

[121] Chief State Councilor, Second State Councilor, and Third State Councilor.

156.

At the sight of my bamboo stick I grow happy and proud.
When I was a child, I liked to ride on it.
After standing behind the window, now it walks in front of me.

157.

All men of the world are foolish.
They know they'll die but don't know how to enjoy themselves.
We who know this spend all day drunk.

158.

Have you ever seen someone rise from the dead?
No one ever said, I came back to life. I've never seen that.
Knowing what we know, we enjoy ourselves in this life.

159.

Did the Yellow River run clear? A holy man was born.[122]
Did all the wise men in the country rise in revolt?
Ah, with whom can we switch this beautiful country?

160.

I snap off a thin willow bough to skewer the fish I caught,
Then cross the rickety bridge to go to the tavern.
Falling apricot blossoms cover the valley, and I lose my way.

---

[122] The water of the Yellow River is said to run clear once every thousand years, when a holy man is born. Here it refers to the Injo Restoration, when King Kwanghaegun was expelled.

161.

The east wind blows lightly, melting piles of snow.
The old faces of the green mountains show themselves in all
    four corners.
But the frost below my ears[123] doesn't melt.

162.

Boss Ch'oi, let's make mugwort pancakes, my coeval Cho, let's
    make flower pancakes.
Let me steam chicken, crab, and early-ripening rice for lunch.
Why worry if we can live like this every day?

**Chang Man**: His other name was Hogo, and his penname was Naksŏ. He was Associate Councilor, Minister of Defense, and Supreme Field Commander during the reign of King Injo. He was appointed Lord of Oksŏng.

163.

Surprised by wind and waves, the boatman sold his boat to buy
    a horse.
Winding mountain roads are more difficult to navigate than a
    waterway.
From now on I will only plow, setting aside the boat and the
    horse.

**Ch'ae Yuhu**: His other name was Paekch'ang, and his penname was Hoju. He passed the civil service examination

---

[123] A metaphor for gray hair under the ears.

during King Injo's reign and became a member of Reading Hall. He was First Academician and Chancellor of the National Academy at the same time. His final government post was Minister of Personnel.

164.

Raw rice wine is good, whether sweet or sour; wine in a bamboo-hooped bottle is better.
Hooray, a gourd ladle is floating in the jar.
Boy, just don't say you have no salted kimchi—bring me some!

**Chŏng T'aehwa**: His other name was Yuch'un, and his penname was Yangp'a. He passed the civil service examination during King Injo's reign and was Chief State Councilor. His posthumous title was Ikhŏn.

165.

I'm sitting up wide awake, though I'm drunk.
Millions of worries bid farewell: goodbye!
Boy, fill my glass. I'm casting off my worries.

**Chŏng Tugyŏng**: His other name was Kunp'yŏng, and his penname was Tongmyŏng. He passed the civil service examination during King Injo's reign and was Vice-Minister of Rites and Deputy Director. His writings were brilliant.

166.

I drain rice wine from a golden jar.
Oh, the boundless pleasure of singing when I'm drunk.

Don't say the sun has set. The moon is rising.

167.

Jun Ping[124] abandoned the world, and the world abandoned him.
Drunkenness is the best of the best, and worldly affairs are the worst of the worst.
Only fresh wind and the bright moon follow me wherever I go.


I liked poetry from my youth and received unmerited love from Tongmyŏng Chŏng Tukyŏng, who called me "Kyŏngjŏngsan," [125] which means, "looking at each other doesn't bore us."
    I fell chronically ill in 1668, didn't go out, closed my door. One day Tongmyŏng came unexpectedly to see me, followed by Hyuwa Im Yuhu and Paeggok Kim Tŭgsin. So I hosted a small drinking party and called some women to play music for us.
    Midway through the party, Tongmyŏng said, excitedly, "When a man is born, a bright spring scene flashes by like lightning. Today's pleasure is worth a generous government

---

[124] 君平, Yan Zun's (嚴遵) other name, was also Chŏng Tukyŏng's other name. Yan Zun was a fortune teller in the Han dynasty. People ignored his prophesies, so he left the world and lived as a fortune teller for more than ninety years. When he earned one hundred nyang, he would close his shop; when he had spent all his money, he would reopen it.

[125] 敬亭山, Jing Ting Mountain, known in antiquity as Zhao Ting Mountain, is in the northern suburbs of Xuancheng, Anhui Province, China. 衆鳥高飛盡 孤雲獨去閑 相看兩不厭 只有敬亭山: "The birds were flying high, and one cloud sailed alone. Only gazing at Jingting Mountain doesn't bore me."

stipend." Hyuwa recited a quatrain, "As Spring ferments winter plum, old wine thickens. Two old men, Tongmyŏng and Paeggok, met with much difficulty. Then glasses, kŏmun'go, the five-string mandolin, clear song. When I gazed, drunkenly, at Mt. Chongnam, snow fell on the peak."

After composing his poem, he said to Tongmyŏng, "The weak go first, so I hope you will lift the kettle with the strength of someone lifting a caldron to pour water into the basin."[126]

Tongmyŏng said, "At the Lanting meeting, those who write poems write poems and those who drink wine drink wine. To enjoy today, it's right that singers sing and dancers dance, so please let me sing." Then he wrote a short lyric and sang it in a loud voice, waving his hand, a big smile on his face. He was a true drunken hermit with white hair and red cheeks.

Hyuwa asked me to answer him. Forgetting myself, I wrote: "When I open the jar on a clear night, wine overflows the amber glass. When three good old writers meet at the same time, a thousand-kyun[127] wild stroke of their brush is strong enough to overthrow a thousand hills and ten-thousand-chang[128]-high peaks." They applauded me, saying it was good.

Manju Hong Sŏggi came later and downed three cups of wine in a row. He pulled Paeggok up by the hand to dance. Tongmyŏng turned to me and said, "How about the pleasure we take at the age of a hundred? I don't regret not seeing the dead, but I do regret them not seeing me. Please record this so

---

[126] 奉匜沃盥, Feng Fei Wah: washing a guest's hands with ladled water to show respect.
[127] A traditional unit of weight: one kyun is thirty kŭn (about six hundred grams).
[128] A traditional unit of length: one chang is ten cha (about thirty centimeters).

that our meeting will be known to future generations." So I wrote this down to show how our elders expressed themselves. P'ungsanhuin Hyŏnmukcha Hong Uhae wrote this.

**Kang Paengnyŏn**: His other name was Suggu, and his penname was Sŏlbong. He won first place in the civil service examination during King Injo's reign and was Honorary Minister of Rites and Academician.

168.

The beautiful face of my youth has aged because of my beloved.
I wonder if he will recognize me when we meet.
I would let anyone draw my face and send it to him.


**Yi Wan**: His other name was Ch'ungji. He passed the national military examination during King Injo's reign and was Second Chief Councilor.

169.

Would the Dongting Lake[129] have been larger if Junshan Mountain[130] was flattened?
The moon would shine brighter if I had cut down the cinnamon trees.
How sad it is to grow old without my wishes coming true.

---

[129] 洞庭湖, Tongjŏng Lake: a shallow lake, China's largest, in northeastern Hunan Province.
[130] 君山, Junshan or Princess's Island in the Dongting Lake derives its name from the legend of the Xiang River goddesses. Once a Taoist retreat, it is less than one square kilometer wide.

**Hŏ Chŏng**: His other name was Chungok, and his penname was Songho. He passed the civil service examination during King Hyojong's reign and was the Royal Secretary-transmitter.

170.

Three-legged crows in the sun, don't fly away. Listen to me.
Among birds, you are the filial Zeng Shen.[131]
Please let my graying parents age slowly.

171.

The moonlight shines like day on a snowy night in Sŏho.[132]
Carefully donning a hakch'ang'ŭi,[133] I go down to the riverbank.
Face to face, I see the feather-clothed fairies on Mt. Penglai.

172.

How can the fence stay intact once the straw thatch is removed?
How can you make it through a long night in an unheated room?
My child babbles, oblivious to the affairs of the world.

**Prince Nangwŏn**, grandson of Sŏnjo and Prince Inhŭng's son. His name was Kan, his other name was Hwasuk, and his penname was Ch'oeraktang.

---

[131] 曾參, Zeng Shen: Refers to Zengzi, an influential Chinese philosopher and disciple of Confucius, famous for his filial piety.
[132] Refers to the area of the Han River from Map'o to Sŏgang in the Chosŏn period.
[133] A traditional jacket with wide sleeves and parted seams. A broad black band was attached to the edges of the white cloth.

173.

Passing Chŏngu Pavilion, I arrive at the leisurely Ch'oeraktang.
My life of geomungo and books is always pleasing.
How can there be an end to the fresh wind and the bright moon?

174.

Mountains stand, and no trace of water
Flowing day and night. How can it stay behind?
I don't know anything about water flowing for a thousand years.

175.

When was the moon born? Who first made wine?
After Liu Ling left the world, Taibai followed him.
Nothing to ask for, and nowhere to go. I'll drink and play alone.

176.

This is due to the king's grace and that is also due to his grace.
Noblemen gathered here, whether you realize it or not.
You need to know this if you want to enjoy peace in the world.

177.

This is Ch'ŏnhyangju.[134] Don't say you don't like it.
After getting drunk today, let's drink again to relieve the hangover.
How can we not get drunk in such a happy time?

---

[134] Wine from the world of hermits, which in literary terms means heavenly fragrance.

178.

The slow waters of Mt. Ch'ŏnpo pass the village of Kŭmgok.
Do you or do you not know why Ongnyudang[135] was built?
If you know the true reason, you'll know it was me.

179.

When I come to Ongnyudang, having heard good things about it,
Only Ongnyu water flows under Mt. Ch'ŏnpo.
Alas, no one here takes pleasure in mountains and rivers.

180.

Mt. Shuyang, where are Boyi and Shuqi?
Who knows why they abandoned their fidelity to the past?
But I have seen the peaceful era of Emperors Yao and Shun.

181.

When after much difficulty I arrive at Lord Jiang's[136] fishing hole,
Mountains and rivers are endless, and my spirit is revived.
I see the noble spirit of every age again.

182.

---

[135] A country house built by Prince Nangwŏn in Kŭmgok.
[136] 姜尙, Jiang Ziya, also known by several other names, was a Chinese nobleman who helped Kings Wen and Wu of Zhou overthrow the Shang in ancient China.

When I pass the Luhan River,[137] Lord Tai's fishing hole appears.
How does the present-day scenery of the Wei River[138] differ from the old days?
I have seen firsthand the prophecy of the jade bead.[139]

183.

The slow waters of Mt. Shuyang are said to flow into the fishing hole.
I want to catch the fish Lord Tai used to catch.
But it's no longer here. And I'm not sure if it will bite.

The above three poems were my responses to the poem King Hyojong wrote at the fishing hole.

184.

The sun and moon are the same and so are mountains and rivers.
But the products of the Ming civilization are gone forever.
Look, fortunes turn. Perhaps I'll see them again.

185.

---

[137] 灤河水, Luanheshui: Luhan River.
[138] 渭水, Wei River: A major river in west-central China's Gansu and Shaanxi Provinces. Lord Jiang fished here for ten years, biding his time.
[139] Lord T'ae fished up a jade bead inscribed with a prophecy referring to the founding of the Zhou dynasty by Kings Wen and Wu, who conquered the Shang.

I travel to Mt. P'ungak[140] behind a piping boy.
Where have the hermits gone? Only a crane's nest remains.
If you meet Chisongzi,[141] please tell him I'm here.

186.

I saunter around mountains and lakes, with nothing to do.
Possessing this portion of nature, I have forgotten every worldly care.
Ah, these great mountains and rivers are my friends.

187.

Royal favor is unlimited, and it continues through the generations.
In this peaceful reign, it's difficult to find a way to repay it.
But my heart will never forget my loyalty to the nation.

188.

If I can cut off only three cha of the withered paulownia[142] rooted in stone,
It will turn into a geomungo all by itself.
But no one will understand the Kosanyusu[143] tune.

---

[140] Another name for Mt. Kŭmkang.
[141] 赤松子: An ancient fairy in the time of Shennong.
[142] A withered upright paulownia was regarded as the best wood for a geomungo.
[143] A tune based on an anecdote concerning Bo Ya and Zhong Ziqi. Bo Ya was good at playing the qin. Zhong Ziqi was good at listening to the qin. When tall mountains inspired Bo Ya's playing, Zhong Ziqi said, "Towering, like Mount Tai!" When flowing water inspired Bo Ya's playing, Zhong Ziqi said, "How vast are the rivers and oceans!" Whatever Bo Ya thought, Ziqi never failed to grasp it. Bo Ya said,

189.

Pine tree, pine tree, why are you planted here?
Why are you here instead of by the stream where mountain water slowly flows?
No one understands how you stay green for so long.

190.

It was dark after sunset—I thought it was midnight.
But it dawned in a flash, and a new day began.
The years go by like running water. Old age saddens me.

191.

After deciding my lot is good,
I won't swap my thatched house for rank and fame.
I'll behave once I leave the secular world.

192.

If you know the laws of nature, you must know the way to Heaven.
The great cause of fidelity and filial duty depends on training the self.
If you have integrity, I think everything will be fine.

193.

If you always practice virtue, you'll know it's your way.

---

"Amazing! Your heart and mine are the same!" When Ziqi died, Bo Ya broke the strings [of his qin] and vowed never to play again. Thus the melody of High Mountains Flowing Water.

If you understand how to restrain your anger, you'll know it's to control passion.
If you treasure learning, you'll know what to keep and what to discard.

194.

If you're discreet when you talk, you'll have no disputes.
If you don't like the life of leisure, you won't suffer from greed.
If you do anything besides this, your learning will come to nothing.

195.

Hey, listen to me. After studying to become a man of virtue,
Who knows when your life will end? Don't quarrel over age.
There will still be days to spare, and I'll devote myself to my studies.

196.

If one is born and learns the laws of nature,
To distinguish right from wrong, he won't envy even Confucius and Mencius.
People say lots of things, but I don't care.

197.

My parents bore me and raised me to be virtuous.
Without them, how could I have been born and grow wise.
I don't think I can repay them for their immense love.

198.

Though our bodies are born separately, don't regard us as two bodies.
We're brothers, with separate shapes but the same spirit.
Brothers, keep this in mind. Respect and love each other.

199.

Everybody knows that men and women are different.
But it's difficult to know this without learning.
Act judiciously, because there is a strict national law.

200.

Youngster, if you know the order everywhere to serve the elderly,
Ignorant commoners can't help but know it, too.
If you want to know morality, there is no other way but to practice it.

201.

Those who are not relatives but remain close are called friends.
If they don't believe in each other, there's no reason for them to be friends.
We're close friends, we gladly accept encouragement to do good.

202.

The people in my hometown are well-mannered; no one is rude.
Though ignorant boys don't know how to behave toward the elderly,
They, too, can learn, since they have the shape of a human.

One day I met Lord Nangwŏn, a royal, at Ch'oeraktang. He gave me a small book titled *Yŏngŏn* and said, "Here I have collected my inmost thoughts when I was at home or traveling and tired and wanted some fun. Please comment on it." I received it politely and stepped back. I read it aloud three times, found no vulgar or debauched pieces, indeed many pieces of high distinction, including several dozen that expressed his love for the king, his desire to repay him for his gratitude, and his wish to be vigilant and act prudently.

Because I can't sing, I don't know whether the tunes and rhythms are appropriate to their different classes. But what he wrote about mountains and waters is truly profound, far-seeing, and free, as if embodying the meaning bequeathed to us by Gouling[144] and Huainan.[145] In songs of gratitude to the king, the sincerity of his loyalty spills wildly over the surface meaning of his text. His self-deprecating words are so precise they seem to belong to the enlightened. In short, all are worthy of being sung and handed down.

Song is a form of poetry. Hence the folk songs of common people, the lyrics of the farm encouragement officers and farmers, were raised to the rank of poems played on pipes and string instruments in villages and across the country to lift people up. Songs cannot be cast off. Ah, Lord Nangwŏn was of noble standing—even the king treated him as ascendant; he had a high position and his children were prosperous; a gold and rhino-hide belt and a sable-and-jade crown illuminated the garden in front of his bright stairs. His enormous wealth and fame led people to compare him to Wansijun.[146]

---

[144] 緱嶺, Gouling, refers to Mt. Gou in Yanshi City.
[145] 淮南, Huainan, a city in Anhui Province.
[146] 萬石君: Literally, "a man with 10,000 shi." Refers to 石奮 Shi Fen of the Han dynasty. He and his four sons each received a salary of 2,000 shi (a traditional unit of measure, about 180 liters); hence

But Lord Nangwŏn was a cautious man, practicing the virtues of a classical scholar who wears cotton clothes. His words came from his upright nature. How can the high esteem they deserve be like the lyrics of farm encouragement officers and farmers? Sadly, we have no custom of collecting songs in this country, and so they must be hidden in a box. But if we let people read this book, wouldn't the vulgar desire of pursuing profit be cured a little in the recitation of the songs in an elongated voice? His love for the king and his prudent ways show no sign of ceasing. I hope he won't hide or refrain from speaking.

Cousin Yŏnan Yi Hajo[147] wrote this in January 1697.

**Nam Kuman** (1629-1711): His other name was Ullo and his penname was Yagch'ŏn. He passed the civil service examination during King Hyojong's reign and was Chief State Councilor. After retirement, he was appointed Honorary Minister.

203.

Has the eastern window dawned? Skylarks are singing.
Isn't the cowherd up yet?
When will he plow the long-furrowed field over the hill?


**Yu Hyŏgyŏn**: He passed the military examination and served as a division commander during King Sukchong's reign.

---

10,000 shi.
[147] Yi Hajo (1664-1700): A civil official in the late Chosŏn period. His other name was Nakpo and his penname was Samsuhŏn. He was the Magistrate of Pup'yŏng.

204.

A fast horse ages into standing still, and a sharp knife rusts.
Merciless time hastens to turn my hair gray.
I fear I may not repay the grace of my benevolent lord.


**Pak T'aebo**: His other name was Sawŏn, and his penname was Chŏngjae. He passed the civil service examination during King Sukchong's reign and was Fourth Advisor in the Office of Special Advisers. He is one of three leaders of Gisa Restoration.

205.

Fire broke out in my heart, and my five viscera burned out of control.
I met Shennong in a dream and asked him for medicine to put out the fire.
There's no medicine, he said, for a fire set by my fidelity and righteous wrath.


**Kim Sŏngch'oe** (1645-1713): A literary man in the late Chosŏn period. His other name was Ch'oeryang and his penname was Illodang. He kept company with Kim Kwanguk, Kim Ch'anghyŏp and Kim Ch'anghŭp brothers. He was the Magistrate of Ch'ŏngju.

206.

I have nothing to do since retiring from government.
I load wine into my small boat and visit Sijung Pavilion.
I think the seagulls flying over the flowering reeds are my

friends.

207.

When I sit down to play geomungo after sobering up,
A crane outside my window joyously flies up and down.
Boy, pour me the rest of the wine, I'm getting excited again.

208.

Friend, please call me when the wine in your house ripens.
I'll call you when the flowers in my house bloom.
I'd like to talk to you about how to forget our worries forever.

**Kim Ch'angŏp** (1658-1721): A literary man and artist in the late Chosŏn period. His other name was Taeyu, his penname was Kajae, and his other penname was Sŏkkyo. He didn't take a government position and lived in his hometown for life, playing geomungo, writing poetry, and hunting.

209.

When I take a nap after plucking the geomungo,
My dog barks at the twig gate and my dear friend comes in.
Boy, bring me raw wine on credit, I'll eat and drink with him.

210.

I rounded up a young hawk that was just one cha tall.
After tying a bell to its tail, I went about with it on my arm.
No boast is greater than this for a man.

211.

If everyone enters government, who will farm?
If doctors cure every disease, why are there cemeteries?
Boy, fill my cup, I'll do as I like.

**Sin Chŏngha** (1680-1715): An official in the late Chosŏn period. His other name was Chŏngbo, his penname was Sŏan, and his other penname was Sŏkho. He passed the civil service examination during King Sukchong's reign and was a remonstrator. He is a literary man under Kim Ch'anghyŏp.

212.

A government position is dear, but is it more precious than my body?
When I spurred the limping donkey to take me home,
A sudden rain washed away the dirt of the secular world.

213.

Undaunted T'aebo Pak,[148] don't be sad about your death.
You alone held fast to three hundred years of moral principles.[149]
Your death makes possible our benevolent king's upcoming restoration.[150]

**Cho Kwanbin** (1691-1757): An official in the late Chosŏn

---

[148] T'aebo Pak (1654-1689) passed the civil service examination during the reign of King Sukjong and was the Magistrate of P'aju.
[149] Three hundred years, the duration of the Chosŏn dynasty until that time.
[150] Refers to King Sukchong's restoration of Queen Inhyŏn.

period. His other name was Kukpo, his penname was Hoehŏn, and his other penname was Kwangjae. He was the son of Cho T'aech'ae, one of the four leaders of Old Doctrine. He passed the civil service examination during King Sukchong's reign and was a minister in the government.

214.

Born human, if you can't be Gao Yao[151] or Hou Ji,[152]
Who else will you envy in our long history?
Boating on the Taihu Lake[153] to enjoy the moon is wise.

215.

Though the general's mansion is magnificent, and the minister's is gorgeous,
Without fame or honor, however rich they may be,
I would rather be a recluse among the green mountains and the water.

---

[151] 皐陶, Gao Yao: Minister of Law for Emperor Shun in prehistorical China, according to tradition. He established the penal code and built prisons.

[152] 后稷, Hou Ji: A legendary figure credited with introducing millet to the Chinese during the Xia dynasty. 契, Xie: An ancient Chinese nobleman, educational administrator, and ancestor of Shang dynasty kings.

[153] 太湖, Taihu in the Yangtze delta, aka Lake Tai or Taihu, is one of the largest freshwater lakes in China. In the Spring and Autumn period, Fan Li (范蠡) was a Chinese military strategist, politician, businessman, and advisor to Goujian, King of Yue. He was known as Tao Zhu Gong (陶朱公) after conquering the state of Wu and then retiring to live in seclusion with his wife Xi Shi, one of the most famous beauties in Chinese history.

## Works of Kings

**King T'aejong** (1367-1422): The third king of the Chosŏn dynasty. His name was Yi Pangwŏn, and his other name was Yudŏk. He greatly contributed in founding the Chosŏn dynasty and strengthened it with his many achievements. He reigned the country from 1400-1418.

216.[154]

What does it matter if I go this way or that?
What does it matter if kudzu vines on Mt. Mansu [155] are tangled up?
I hope we become entangled like that and live for a hundred years.

**King Hyojong** (1619-1659): The 17th King of the Chosŏn dynasty. His name was Ho, his other name was Chŏngyŏn, his penname was Chugo, and he was King Injo's second son. He was sent to Shenyang as a hostage during the Manchu War, where he lived for eight years. He planned a northern campaign and appointed Song Siyŏl and Yi Wan to important positions but couldn't accomplish his plan. He reigned the country from 1649-1659.

217.[156]

---

[154] Yi Pangwŏn sang this sijo to test Chŏng Mongju's loyalty to the Koryŏ dynasty. This is commonly called "Song of What Matters." Sijo #8 above is Chŏng's answer to him.
[155] A mountain outside Kaesŏng, the Koryo dynasty's capital.
[156] Written when Grand Prince Pongnim was taken hostage during the Manchu War in 1636. Ch'ŏngsŏngnyŏng and Ch'ohagu are place

Did we cross Ch'ŏngsŏnnyŏng Pass? Where is Ch'ohagu?
This barbarian wind is so cold, and what a gloomy rainstorm!
I hope someone will describe my situation and send it to my beloved.

218.

Will Choch'ŏllo[157] rust or Okhakwan[158] empty?
Where has Emperor Sungjŏng[159] of the Great Ming gone?
This three-hundred-year fidelity[160] seems like a dream.

219.

Ah, I wish I wasn't human. Letting feathers grow on my body
And soaring lightly into the ninety thousand li distant sky,
I want to look down on the Royal Palace, where my king lives.

**King Sukchong** (1661-1720): The 19th King of the Chosŏn dynasty. His name was Sun, his other name was Myŏngbo. He implemented the Uniform Land Tax Law (Taedongpŏp) and expanded territory by erecting a national boundary monument on Mt. Paektu.

---

names on the way to Shenyang, where he was held.
[157] 朝天路: The road that special envoys took to pay tribute to Chinese emperors.
[158] 玉河館: A lodge in Beijing for Chosŏn envoys.
[159] 崇禎帝 The Chongzhen Emperor, personal name Zhu Youjian, was the seventeenth and last emperor of the Ming dynasty (also the last Han Chinese emperor), reigning from 1627 to 1644. "Chongzhen," the era name of his reign, means "honorable and auspicious."
[160] See note #149.

220.

Autumn water is sky-blue, and the king's boat floats on the water.
Our old anxiety dissolves at the sound of the t'ungso[161] and the drum.
Let's enjoy this peaceful reign with all the people.

## Six Commoner Poets

**Chang Hyŏn** (1613- ): A translator in the mid-Chosŏn period. As a paternal first cousin once removed of Huibin Chang, he was the head translator during Sukchong's reign. He accompanied Prince Sohyŏn and Grand Prince Pongnim when they were taken to Ching China as hostages after the Manchu War.

221.

My wretched beloved, after the sunset at Amnok River,
Why are you heading for ten thousand li distant Yanjing?
Please come back soon, when the spring grass turns green.

**Chu Ŭisik**: His other name was Towŏn and his penname was Namgok. He passed the military examination and was a kyoryŏn'gwan (military officer) and magistrate of Ch'irwŏn.

222.

Don't stand on your toes to say the sky is high.

---

[161] A six-holed bamboo flute, a traditional musical instrument.

Don't stomp on the earth to say it's thick.
I'll be careful, though earth and sky are thick.

223.

A boy stopped outside the window and said today is the new year.
When I opened the east window, the same sun had risen.
Boy, come to me in the next world, for the sun is always the same.

224.

If I speak out, people call me vulgar. If I'm silent, they call me foolish.
People laugh at the poor and envy the rich.
Under Heaven, it's difficult to speak out.

225.

Walking aimlessly in my old sick body,
I'll plough a field on the self-risen mountain.
I hope its yield will be enough for my survival.

226.

After finding wild jade on Mt. Jing,[162] I went looking for people.
Who knows what's inside it? Its exterior is stone.
Never mind. Live like a stone, whose value no one knows.

---

[162] 荆山: The Jingshan or Jing Mountains in Nanzhang County, Hubei Province, China.

227.

When I think of my life, it's just a sliver of a dream.
Good things, bad things: dreams in a dream.
Yes, life is like a dream. What can I do but enjoy it?

228.

I climbed Mt. Shuyang to die of hunger.
I plucked the fern not to eat
But to straighten it, for I hate how it coils.

229.

The fish that swallowed Qu Yuan's[163] loyal spirit became a whale in Cai Shiji.[164]
Carrying Li Bai[165] on his back, the fish soared into the sky.
New fish are born. What does it matter if I catch and boil them?

230.

Because that king didn't know what was in his loyal vassal's heart,
Everyone grieved for a thousand years in the nether world.

---

[163] 屈原: Qu Yuan, a Chinese poet and politician who lived during the Warring States period, is remembered for his patriotism and contributions to classical poetry.
[164] 采石江: Cai Shiji, on the Yangtze River's east bank, in Maanshan, Anhui Province, China. Legend has it that Li Bai, a Tang dynasty poet regarded as a genius and romantic figure who brought new life to traditional forms, drowned there, drunkenly trying to embrace the moon.
[165] 李謫仙: Refers to Li Bai.

Because Bigan[166] revealed his heart, what grudge can he harbor?

231.

Tanyu[167] is good, but Xiashangzhou[168] is much better.
Which age is comparable to this one?
I don't know which age will do, for Yaoshun[169] illuminated the world.

I received a couple of Lord Chu Towŏn's[170] new songs and regret not getting the rest. One day Mr. Pyŏn Hwasuk showed them to me. After three readings, I find the lyrics fair, not harsh—the product of an affectionate heart and poetic skill. If the examiner of folkways had collected these songs, they would have displayed them as poems.

When I tried to imagine what kind of person the writer was, I decided he couldn't be a man of this world. Ah! He's not only good at this, but polite and humble, his mind, calm and serene. He has the air of a gentleman.

---

[166] 比干: A prominent Chinese figure during the Shang dynasty. He was a son of King Wen Ding, and an uncle of the last Shang king, Di Xin. Annoyed by Bi Gan's advice to mend his ways, Di Xin ordered Bigan's execution by the extraction of his heart to check his fidelity.
[167] 陶虞: Emperors Yao and Shun were referred to interchangeably. 陶唐: Taotang was Yao's clan name, and 有虞 Youyu was Shun's lineage name.
[168] 夏商周: Refers to the Xia, Shang, and Zhou dynasties in ancient China.
[169] Refers to Emperors Yao and Shun.
[170] Refers to Chu Ŭisik. Towŏn was his other name. He passed his military exams during the reign of Hyŏnjong and was the Magistrate of Ch'irwŏn.

Namp'anop'o wrote this in early May 1728.

**Kim Samhyŏn**: A commoner poet during King Sukjong's reign and Chu Ŭisik's son-in-law.

232.

Did you grow old, little knowing that growing old is sad?
Spring sunlight is fleeting, gray hair sprouts by itself.
But the heart of my youth hasn't shriveled yet.

233.

If you want to seize the March of green willows,
You should pull out your gray hairs to bind them tight.
I failed again to do so this year and let it go.

234.

Waking from a light sleep in the pine forest, I look around with drunken eyes.
White seagulls sail in and out of the port at sunset.
Ah, the scenery of this land is truly boundless.

235.

Don't pine for fame and honor: glory and shame are half-and-half.
Don't covet riches and ranks, or you will face a crisis.
We are men of leisure, we have nothing to fear.

236.

Four men[171] resting at leisure on a huge rock.
Can I finally hear a Zizhiqu[172] tune today?
Later, I will be added to them to make five old men.

237.

If my soul, mixed with wine, flows into my beloved
And searches out every corner of his nine-fold intestines,
I'd like to set fire to his heart, which forgot me and moved on
    to another.

**Kim Sŏnggi** (1649-1724): His other name was Chaho, and his other pennames were Nangong, Ŏong, and Chŏŭn. A commoner poet and master player of geomungo in the late Chosŏn dynasty.

238.

Leaving the world for the mountains and rivers, I befriended a
    white gull.
Afloat in my fishing boat, I play a jade pipe.
I think this is my only joy in the world.

239.

Winter is gone and spring is here.

---

[171] 商山四皓, "Shangshan Four Hao: Four doctors who lived in Shangshan to escape the Qin chaos: Dong Yuangong Tang Ning, Xia Huanggong Cui Guang, Qi Li Ji Wu Shi, and Zhou Li.
[172] 紫芝歌, Zizhiqu: Composed of the four characters named Shanghao Four Hao, who lived in Shangshan (Dongyuangong, Qiliji, Xiahuanggong, and Li).

The valleys and peaks are bedecked in green.
Boy, launch my boat on the river and bring me my fishing rod.

240.

With nothing to do, I went to Sŏho.
Only gulls were flying over the white sand and clean river.
Somewhere a fisherman's song was adding to my joy.

241.

White gulls sleeping among water peppers, don't wake up and fly away.
With nothing to do, I, too, am a guest in nature.
Since no one visits me, I'll play after you.

242.

Those who live in dust and dirt,[173] please listen to me.
They say riches and honors are good,
But priceless mountains and rivers are better

243.

Holding my bamboo cane, I shake off the red dust, put on my straw shoes,
Shoulder a Korean zither, and enter the deep mountain valley.
A crane that lost its partner cries somewhere beyond the clouds.

244.

I cut off a bough of blossoms from the plum tree growing in

---

[173] The secular world.

a jade pot.
The flowers are nice, but their mellow fragrance is better.
Leave them alone. No need to throw cut flowers away.

245.

If you catch an unbridled flying horse
And feed it millet porridge and steamed beans until it grows
    fat,
It won't stay, thanks to its wild nature.


From an early age I was crazy for songs, and when our royal court opened I collected works by famous scholar officials and common people alike. Kim Sŏnggi's scores were delivered to me occasionally, but few knew his body of work. I looked for it in vain, which saddened me.

    I met Sŏho Kim Chungnyŏ at Mun Ukchae's[174] house the other day, and Kim was Ŏŭn's[175] best friend. I said, "Because you have known him from youth, you must have written down his songs and kept them. Can you show them to me?"

    He replied, "I've been with Ŏŭn in the countryside for a dozen years, recording everything that poured out of his heart when he got excited. Many pieces move people, but the ignorant don't appreciate them, so I keep them in a box, waiting for a dilettante. But from what you say I think they will eventually be known around the world." Then he gave them to me. I've recited them three times, taking great pleasure in their lyrical expressions about nature, feeling as though I had suddenly left this world.

---

[174] Details about this person are unknown.
[175] Kim Sŏnggi's penname.

Ŏŭn was a man of leisure, freely wandering the world, his rhythms, mysterious and profound. He liked mountains and rivers, built a house by Sŏgang,[176] and gave himself the penname Ŏŭn.[177] On clear mornings and moon-bright nights he would sit by the fishing hole plucking the geomungo or stroll by the fog-shrouded river playing the six-holed bamboo flute. He forgot the affairs of the world, flirting with seagulls and gazing at fish, and left his body. Hence he enjoyed what was enjoyable and sang his lyrics well.

Namp'anop'o wrote this on March 16, 1728.

**Kim Yugi**: A commoner poet in the late Chosŏn period. His other name was Taejae, and he was from Namwŏn.

246.

Chronically ill, I left the secular world
And forgot right and wrong, honor and disgrace.
Falconry is my only leisure activity.

247.

Born male, if I can't rise in the world and gain fame,
I'll put it all aside and grow old doing nothing.
Nothing trivial will weigh on my mind.

248.

Doomed to live but seventy years, not a hundred,
I wish to be spared suffering, nakedness, hunger,

---

[176] The western part of the Han River Basin, where the Pongwŏn Stream and Han River meet; also called Sŏho.
[177] The literal meaning of Ŏŭn is fisherman hermit.

And disease, and have many descendants.

249.

Plum blossoms fluttering in spring wind, don't show off your shapeliness.
Regard the tall pine trees and green bamboo in midwinter.
No need to change your high, upright faithfulness.

250.

When did Tang Yu[178] live and who were Kongmaeng?[179]
Simple customs, courtesy, and music—all is chaos.
I, a lowly scholar, beat time, singing a sad song.

251.

When I climb Mt. Tai and look down at the four seas,
The world is wide and boundless.
What I see today is man's upright spirit.

252.

I am neither a loyal servant nor a filial son, and I committed many sins,
Leading a meager life while achieving nothing special.
And yet I'm sad to grow old in this peaceful reign.

253.

---

[178] A combination of Tang Yao and Yu Shun, referring to the days of Yao and Shun.
[179] Refers to Confucius and Mencius.

Let's go river fishing today and mountain climbing tomorrow.
Let's fry flower fan cake the day after tomorrow and do kangsin[180] the day after that.
Please bring your own food for the archery competition two days after tomorrow.

254.

When I sit back against the banister to play the jade pipe,
Plum blossoms flutter down in Jiangcheng[181] in May.[182]
I'll play a melody of unification on Emperor Shun's pentachord.

255.

Auspicious star and cloud appear, and the sun and moon shine bright.
The manners and music of Three Sovereigns, the culture of Five Emperors.
I'll vint a fine peace wine from the Four Seas and get drunk with everyone.

---

[180] A meeting of the members of the local kye, a private traditional fund popular among Koreans, who chip in a modest amount of money and take turns receiving shares of it as a lump sum. They usually have a drinking party to strengthen their bonds.

[181] 江城, Jiangcheng: Refers to Wuhan, the capital of Hubei Province, China.

[182] These lines come from Li Bai's (李白) poem, "Listening to Haung He Upstairs with Shi Lang Zongqin (与史郎中钦听黄鹤楼上吹笛)": "Jade flutes play in the Yellow Crane Tower, and plum blossoms drop in Jiangcheng in May (黃鶴樓上吹玉笛, 江城五月落梅花).

Mr. Kim Taejae[183] is a famous singer. When I visited his house in 1716, I took a book from an open box and read his new songs. When he asked me to edit them, I replied, "The lyrics express very well your heart and their rhythms are excellent. These are outstanding scores. How can I add anything with my meager talent?" After talking for a while, I returned home.

He was dead within a couple of years, and Cao Zijina's[184] loss was truly felt. Thus I collected his posthumous works to be spread around the world and handed down forever.

Namp'anop'o wrote this on March 16, 1728.

**Kim Ch'ŏnt'aek**: A commoner poet in the late Chosŏn period and editor of *Songs of the Green Hills*. His other name was Paekham, and Isuk was his other courtesy name. He was a bandit control official during the reign of King Sukchong.

256.

Because glory and shame go hand in hand, I don't care about wealth and fame.
I shall become the master of myself in this most beautiful land
And come and go at sunset, with my fishing pole on my shoulder.

---

[183] Refers to Kim Yugi. Taejae was his penname.
[184] 曹子建, Cao Zijian: 曹植, Cao Zhi's other name. A prince and an accomplished poet in the state of the Wei in the Three Kingdoms period of China. His poetic style, revered during the Jin, Southern, and Northern dynasties, came to be known as the Jian'an style. "洛神賦 Luo Shen Fu Ode to the Nymph of the Luo River" is his most famous poem, which depicts his sorrow by the Luo River, carrying the remains of Zhen Huan, the woman he loved. He loved her but she married Cao Yan, his and Emperor Wei Wen's older brother. But she suffered the Emperor's delusional jealousy and was killed, falsely accused by a royal concubine.

257.

White gull, don't be surprised by my questions.
Where did you leave all the good scenic spots?
If you tell me in detail, I'll go there to play with you.

258.

White gulls, playfully mixing in threes and fives,
Wearing the glow of evening in the depths of the blossoming reeds,
How could you be so absorbed you didn't know I was coming?

259.

I planted five grains on a slope of Mt. Nam.
May the harvest not come up short, leaving no spare food after eating.
I have no other desire for wealth and fame.

260.

I scattered cucumber seeds on the sunlit side below the fence,
Piled earth over them, weeded, and watered them with rain.
Truly, I think Dongling's cucumber field[185] is here.

261.

---

[185] 東陵, Dongling, 邵平, Shao Ping (year of birth and death is unknown): A historical figure from the late Qin and early Han dynasties. During the Qin dynasty, he was named Dongling Hou. When the Hans destroyed Qin, Hou became a commoner, who grew melons outside the southeastern Bacheng Gate in Changan City.

Loading what remains of my rural excitement onto the crippled donkey,
I return cheerfully along a familiar road in the mountain valley.
Boy, prepare books and geomungo. I'll spend the rest of the day with them.

262.

If you want to rise into the cloudy sky, how can you do so without wings?
If you want to go to Pongdao,[186] where will you find a boat and pole?
I'd rather become a lord of the forest and forget the world.

263.

No disgrace in satisfaction, and no danger if you know when to stop.
It's best to quit if you succeed in making a name for yourself.
All government officials, please be careful.

264.

Swift horses grow old in the stable, fine swords rust in the sheath.
Helpless, I could not acquire the cherished will of a man.
White hairs flutter under my ears, which saddens me.

265.

Drawing a long sword and sitting down again, I realize

---

[186] 蓬島, Peng Island refers to Mt. Penglai.

My willful heart became Handan's walk.[187]
Stop it, that's my fate, too. No use in talking about it.

266.

Nothing better than a cup of wine for wealth and fame in life.
Only flowers by the road for artistic taste after death.
No reason to stay sober in this peaceful reign.

267.

Don't decline the cup I offer in order to drink less wine.
Isn't it a good season when flowers bloom and birds sing?
Ah, who knows who will be my partner for flower viewing next
    year?

268.

Thirty days in a month—how many days will you be drunk?
The days I hold a cup are truly mine.
When they're gone, whose days will they become?

269.

Is there any man who became youthful again after growing old?
Nothing from antiquity about anyone growing young again.
That's why we always get drunk and play.

---

[187] 邯鄲步, Handanbu: If you recklessly imitate another's skill you may lose your way. The idiom comes from a story about a boy from Yan country, who imitated the gait of the Zhao people in Handan, the capital of the country. But he forgot his own gait before he learned theirs, and had to crawl back to his country.

270.

It makes me sad to think about life
In fleeting moments at the wayfarer's inn, occupied with my worries.
No reason not to enjoy myself to live several hundred years or do something great.

271.

People of the world, please listen to me.
Is youth always the same? Does gray hair turn black?
How can we not enjoy our finite life?

272.

Moon rises over the plum-blossoming window, clean wind in the lane among bamboos.
I play two or three tunes on my modest geomungo.
Drunkenly leaning into the flower garden, I dream of a peaceful reign.

273.

I wake late from a nap and open my drunken eyes.
The flowers that opened in the night rain give off a mellow fragrance.
I like the clean taste of a house in the mountains.

274.

I climb Mt. Tai and look around.
The roads of the world are complex and quite rough.

Thus Ruan Ji[188] cried on a dead-end street.

275.

Emperor Yao's sun and moon, Emperor Shun's sky and earth—all the same.
But why have the things of the world become so different?
I grieve for the lateness of my birth.

276.

After casting off all painful and anxious-making things,
I enjoy myself leisurely in this peaceful reign.
Somehow I'll get along, thanks to the saints' moral influence.

277.

An auspicious cloud fell on Mt. Ni[189] and a great saint[190] was born.
He succeeded the old saints and taught many people. How great was his virtue!
It was Confucius who synthesized all the saints' teachings.

278.

---

[188] 阮籍, Ruan Ji (210-263), courtesy name Sizong, was a Chinese musician and poet who lived in the late Eastern Han dynasty and the Three Kingdoms period of Chinese history. He was one of the Seven Sages of the Bamboo Grove. Ruan Ji used to ride alone in a carriage to calm his anger and then return, after wailing on a dead-end street.

[189] 尼山, Mount Ni: A hill about thirty km southeast of Qufu in Shandong Province, China, traditionally regarded as the birthplace of Confucius.

[190] Refers to Confucius.

Suppressing one's desires and heeding the law of nature is the
 spirit of the autumn sky.
Who understands the words of others and cultivates the great
 spirit of every age?
I think Mencius expanded the natural law, which earlier saints
 had left undeveloped.

279.

Shiwi [191] Du's loyalty and fidelity can compete with the
 brightness of the sun and moon.
With no place to lay down my will on life's rough roads and
 rugged passes,
I record his boundless loyalty in this piece of a poem.

280.

Yue Fei's[192] liver and gall are incorruptible signs of loyalty and
 filial piety.
What were the four characters on his back?[193]
A little sunlight from the Song dynasty, on a southern bough,
 gleamed in my heart.

281.

---

[191] 拾遺, Retrieval (Government): The poet Du Fu was appointed to this post in the Tang dynasty; his responsibilities included distracting the emperor.

[192] 鵬舉, Pengju: courtesy name of 岳飛 Yue Fei, a Chinese military general, calligrapher, and poet who lived during the Southern Song dynasty.

[193] When the Jin invaded the Southern Song dynasty, Young Yue Fei volunteered for the army. His mother wrote on his back the four characters of 精忠報國 (serve one's country with one's utmost will), which became his credo.

Under the northern twig gate, after dark, Wen Tianxiang[194] was miserable!
His black hair turned gray during the eight-year hardship of the Yuan dynasty.[195]
I still mourn his calm and stoic death.

282.

After building the tall Epang Palace[196] inside the long walls in a thousand-li fertile field,
I tried to hold on to the dream I harbored at that moment.
Alas, it became a thing of the past. Who can I blame for that?

283.

Zhunagzi worked much too hard for nothing.
No use in comparing a quail to a roc.
Stop, all things are different. No comparison will do.

284.

---

[194] 文天祥, Wen Tianxiang, Duke of Xinguo, was a Chinese poet and politician in the last years of the Southern Song dynasty.
[195] Wen, an envoy to the Yuan dynasty, was imprisoned, escaped, rearrested, and imprisoned again in Yanjing, where he suffered for eight years before he died.
[196] 阿房宫: The Epang Palace in western Xi'an, Shaanxi Province, China, was a palace complex built by Emperor Qin Shi Huang.

He Jizhen[197] received Kianghu[198] as a special gift from the Emperor.
What excuse could he use to give it up?
Ah, this land of mine is not bound by anything.

285.

Tugging the reins, they turned a deaf ear to all entreaties and entered Mt. Shouyang,
Where they died of hunger, refusing to eat Zhou's food.
They held out to the end only to turn the rebel's heart.


Mr. Kim Isuk's voice was renowned throughout the land for washing away all the shabbiness of vulgar songs. He would sing a new one, his voice loud and clear, and he composed dozens of songs, which he left to the world for boys to learn how to sing. His lyrics were beautiful and reasonable. The voiced and voiceless tunes of the songs and their pitches naturally correspond to the rhythm. They could compete with Lord Songgang's new songs for superiority. Kim was not only an excellent singer but a superb writer.
　　Ah, a good appraiser of folklore should collect these lyrics and keep them in the music bureau to be used at the local and national levels. They should not be left as low-class

---

[197] 季眞 賀知章, He Zhizhang (659~744), courtesy name Jizhen, was a Chinese poet and scholar-official born in Yongxing. *On Returning Home* is a wistful, nostalgic work He composed on his return to his home village at the age of 85, when Emperor Xuanzong allowed him to retire in 744.

[198] 鏡湖, Kianghu: Another name for 鑑湖, Jinghu Lake. According to legend, Huangdi threw the mirror into the lake, which is also known as Long or Qinghu Lake, located 1.5 kms. southwest of Shaoxing, Zhejiang Province, China.

literature. Why let Kim compose deplorable songs of Yen and Zhao and sing his grievances?

    These songs use words like rivers and lakes, forests, wander, and recluse, and repeat them. They don't stop lamenting, reflecting the decaying world.

    Hŭgwa[199] wrote this in March 1728.

## Three Ladies

**Hwang Chini** (1502 - 1567?): A famous gisaeng in the mid-Chosŏn period. Her real name was Chin, Myŏngwŏl (Bright Moon) was her professional name, and she was considered one of the Three Best at Songdo (another name for Kaesŏng) along with Sŏ Kyŏngdŏk and Pagyŏn Fall.

286.

Green stream in the green mountain, don't boast of your easy flowing.
Once you reach the blue sea, it isn't easy to return.
How about resting when the bright moon fills the empty mountain?

287.

I want to cut out the middle of the long midwinter night
And fold it into coils to keep under the blanket of the spring wind.
On the night my beloved comes, I will unfold its every bend and curve.

---

[199] The penname of Chŏng Raekyo.

288.

When did I, betraying our faith, cheat on my beloved
So that he refuses to visit me at moonless midnight?
What can I do with the sound of falling leaves in the autumn
    wind?

**So Paekchu**: A gisaeng in Pyŏngyang during King Kwanghae's reign. Details of her life are unknown.

289.

After meeting the minister, I came to believe everything.
I'm afraid that in his naivete he might get sick.
He says this and that. We will enjoy a long life together.

**Maehwa**

290.

Spring has returned to the old stump of a plum tree.
Its flowers will likely open on the boughs where they emerged.
But spring snow flutters dizzily, and they hesitate to open.

**Writers Whose Dates Are Unknown**

**Yim Chin**

291.

Placing the loose stringed bow on my arm, with a sword on my

side,
I lay my head on a quiver beside Ch'ŏrong Fortress.[200]
At the sounds of "Did you see it?" and "I saw it," I can't fall asleep.

## Yi Chungjip

292.

Who says I'm old? Is an old man like this?
I'm happy to see a flower, I laugh at a glass.
What can I do with my gray hair fluttering in the spring wind?

**Yi Ch'ong** (? -1504): A royal descendant. King Taejong was his great-grandfather. His other name was Paekwŏn, and his penname was Sŏhojuin.

293.

I have become useless—the world discarded me.
I lie down after sweeping my old house in Sŏho[201] again.
Though I'm free, I'm sorry not to see my beloved.

I collected all the available songs of famous ministers, scholars, commoner poets, and ladies from the end of the Koryŏ dynasty to our royal court. I recorded every song, though some

---

[200] A fortress in Mt. Maengsan, P'yŏngannam Province, generally used as a metaphor for an invincible fortress.
[201] A place name for part of the Han River from Map'o to Sŏgang in the Chosŏn dynasty.

were not considered outstanding. Some writers were not worthy of inclusion, but I included their songs if they were good.

**Anonymous**

294.

What will my thoughts of my beloved become after I die?
Though the mulberry field may become the blue sea,[202]
My loyal heart for my beloved will never change.

295.

Snow and rain fall on the crows, which look whitish black.
How can night-shining clouds and moon-bright balls be dark even at night?
My loyal heart for my beloved knows no change.

296.

The stream that wept last night has flowed on, crying sadly.
Now I think my beloved must have been in tears when he sent it.
I would leave, weeping, for the stream to flow back to my beloved.

297.

Growing old and sick, I cry toward the North.[203]

---

[202] An idiom for a sea change.
[203] Refers to the place where the king lives.

Who doesn't have the beloved in their thoughts?
But only I keep him in mind on a long moon-bright night.

298.

Because my beloved considered me, I believed him completely.
But for whom has his affection moved onto?
I wouldn't be so sad, if he had hated me from the start.

299.

Has yesterday's black hair really turned gray?
Who is that old man with the gaunt face in the mirror?
If my beloved asks, "Who are you?" I'll say it's me.

300.

I think of this and that: so many futile thoughts!
Did I live this life of bad karma, because I wanted to?
The reason I'm still alive is to see my beloved.

301.

Green mountains, don't laugh at me. White clouds, don't make fun of me.
I still love to walk with my gray hair in this dusty world.
I'd like to leave only after repaying the boundless favor of my king.

302.

Flowers and bamboos, don't laugh at me.
I've never forgotten my old pledge to return to nature.
I'd like to return only after repaying the boundless favor of our

king.

303.

I have so much to do, with spring arriving in the rivers and lakes.
I mend the net, and boys plow the fields.
When will we dig up the medicinal herbs sprouting on the mountain?

304.

When I close the book and open the window, I see a boat floating down the river.
The white gulls flying in and out of the scene—what are their intentions?
Ah, I will play after you, not for worldly fame

305.

Rain sprinkles the pond, dusk lingers in the willow trees.
The empty boat is moored, but the boatman is nowhere to be seen.
The gull that lost its mate flies back and forth in the twilight.

306.

The piper's pleasing sounds make me hasten to open the bamboo window.
In the drizzle a boy is seated on the back of an ox by the long bank.
Boy, bring me my fishing pole: Spring has come to the rivers and lakes.

307.

Boy, bring the net, load it onto the fishing boat,
And filter the raw alcohol to pour into the wine jar.
Don't launch the boat onto the water yet, we'll wait for the moon to rise.

308.

Night comes on the autumn river and the tide is cold.
I cast my fishing line—no fish bites.
I row the empty boat home, loading up the indifferent moonlight.

309.

Is that a cuckoo singing? Is that green a willow forest?
Two or three houses in the fishing village appear and disappear in the dust.
The sound of rowing in the dust makes me less self-centered.

*The above poems are about rivers and lakes.*

310.

Leaving riches and honors to others in the world,
I lie down leisurely near the silent mountains and rivers.
My fate? The wild greens sprouting on their own in the spring rain.

311.

Green mountains are silent, flowing waters, shapeless.

No one besides Wang Qiao[204] and Chisongzi[205] knows me.
What fool will dare to ask me to come by or not?

312.

Only the white gull and I know the twelve peaks of Mt.
  Ch'ŏngnyang.[206]
The white gull will not turn wild, but peach blossoms are
  unreliable.
Peach blossoms, don't leave. I don't want any fishermen to
  know this.

*The poems above are about forests.*

313.

Peaceful times, and I live a life of leisure.
Save for the rooster's crowing in the green bamboo grove,
What friend will wake me from my deep auspicious dream?

314.

The boys went off to pick medicinal herbs, and the bamboo
  pavilion is empty.
Who will pick up the scattered Go stones and put them back
  in the box?
Drunk, propped up against the pine tree, I don't know how

---

[204] 王喬: A Taoist hermit, who skillfully played the mouth organ with seventeen bamboo pipes, producing the sound of the phoenix.
[205] 赤松子: A fairy in ancient Chinese mythology—the god of rain, who later became a hermit.
[206] 淸凉山: A mountain in Pongwha, in North Kyŏngsang Province.

time passes.

*The above poems are about leisure.*

315.

A red-necked mountain pheasant, a peregrine hawk perched on the roost,
And a white heron peeking at a fish in the harrowed field in front of my house—
Without you, it's hard for me to spend a day inside the thatched cottage.

316.

A guest arrives in a casual cloth, the host greets him without his horsehair hat,
And they play Go and Korean chess, in the pavilion of ten arm-sized trees.
Boy, filter the raw wine. Even a cucumber side dish is acceptable.

317.

The early morning rain has stopped. Boys, get out of bed.
The ferns on the back mountain must already be up.
Please pick them early today so I can make a side dish of them.

318.

I borrowed grains and got some fish.
My wine is mellow, and the moon is bright on the mountain.
Flowers bloomed, and I have my geomungo. I'll call friends to

play.

319.

Don't bring the straw mat. I can sit on the fallen leaves.
Don't light a pine torch: the moon that set yesterday is rising.
Boy, don't say you don't have raw wine and greens. Please bring
  them.

*The above poems are about pleasures in the field.*

320.

I have forsaken the garrulous world and entered nature.
A furrow in a rough field and eight hundred mulberry trees are
  all I have.
My income is small but I live without a care in the world.

321.

Loyalty is the most important virtue, but it led me to blame my
  beloved.
Alas! What can I do with my lot in life?
I'd rather become the owner of rivers and lakes and forget the
  world.

322.

Who goes to the field on a rainy day? Close the twig gate and
  feed the cow.
The rainy season is always like this. Take care of the plows and
  tools.
Let's rest. We'll plow the long-furrowed field when the sky

clears.

323.

In my bamboo hat and straw raincoat, I hoe in the drizzle,
Weeding a field in the mountains, then lie down in the shade.
A shepherd driving cattle and sheep rouses me from sleep.

324.

Why do chestnuts fall in the valley of red-dimpled jujubes
And crabs fall into the rice stubble?
The sieve paddler comes when wine ripens. How can I resist
    drinking?

325.

Early rice plants bowed their heads and young radishes grew
    fat.
Why do fish bite the hook and crabs collapse?
The clean taste of a farmhouse is good enough for me.

326.

Why do I need these silk clothes to ward off the cold?
What does it matter if wild greens fill my empty stomach?
They're good enough, if I don't have other worries.

327.

If I have no worries, riches and honors don't matter.
If I'm carefree, what if others laugh at me?
Ah, I prefer to live within my means.

328.

Because I wear my own clothes and lie down in my own house,
I don't hear dirty talk and have no disputes.
I think my lot is to live a hundred years like this.

329.

Living recklessly, I achieved nothing.
Scant riches and honors, messy worldly affairs.
Somehow I can live on a couple of cups of wine a day.

330.

These words, those words—all disturbing.
Having or buying wine, I fill the deep cup to the brim.
It's good not to be sobered every day.

331.

If you're foolish, stay foolish to the end. If you're mad, go
    utterly mad.
You're foolish and mad, educated and ignorant.
You've come to nothing oscillating between this and that.

332.

Worldly affairs are messy and entangled, like leftover bits of
    hemp.
I crumple and air them out, I'd like to ignore them.
Boy, play the drum joyfully. I'll hum along.

*The above poems are about freeing one's heart from anxieties.*

333.

How can it be otherwise, being what it is?
It is so this way and that.
I can't help but sigh, being what it is.

334.

I hum merry songs and beat the drum.
I come close to matching kung, sang, kag, ch'i, and wu,[207]
But it's completely out of tune. I guffaw.

*The above poems concern anxiety over worldly things.*

335.

With a bottle of wine, I finally washed away
My old worries, which even the waters of the wide sea couldn't remove.
I know that's why Li Bai never sobered up.

336.

I enjoy liquor, though I know it's a maddening drug.
Putting ten thousand mals[208] of worries into one ch'on of my bowels,
I'd like to forget even the moments I passed out drunk.

---

[207] The traditional five notes in East Asian music.
[208] Traditional units of measure: one mal is about eighteen liters; one ch'on is about three cm.

*The above poems are about relieving worries.*

337.

Do you have two or three lives and four or five bodies?
With a borrowed body and a new lease on life
You only work for your life. When will you play?

338.

Even if you live to be a hundred, how much is that?
Little of it remains if you remove the sick and anxious days.
How in a life of less than a hundred years can we refrain from playing?

*The above poems are about playing and finding pleasure.*

339.

White herons nodding on the sandy beach among red water pepper flowers,
Do you keep bending up and down because you can't fill your stomach?
If you enjoy a life of leisure, what good is it to grow fat?

340.

Kites snatching mice, don't boast of being full.
Do the skinny, hungry cranes by the clear river envy you?
When I'm at leisure, what does it matter if I'm not fat?

*The above poems satirize a busy life.*

341.

Don't act vilely toward others for your pleasure.
Don't do anything that isn't right, just because others do it.
We'll follow our nature and do as we like.

342.

Consider whether what you hear or see is reasonable or not.
If reasonable, follow it. If not, quit it.
If you can discern what people mean, there will be no dispute.

343.

Though some do me harm, I won't argue with them.
If I can bear them, that's my virtue. If I argue, I'm no different than they are.
I won't argue with them, because they're wrong.

*The above poems are about cultivating the mind.*

344.

Don't argue over why crows are black and herons are white.
They're uniformly black and white.
Because we're ospreys and cranes, we're neither black nor white.

345.

I'm afraid of getting hurt, when I try to be decent.
I'm afraid of being deceived, when I try to be generous.
If I'm generous outside and decent inside, I won't be hurt or deceived.

*The above poems are about living comfortably.*

346.

With a pip'a[209] on my shoulder, I lean against the jade banister.
Peach blossoms fall in the east wind and drizzle.
Spring birds sing in many tones, sad as spring departs.

347.

Birds, don't be sad about the falling flowers.
It's not their fault when they scatter in the wind.
Why envy spring's depredations, which say, "I'm leaving?"

*The above poems are about missing the passing spring.*

348.

To say a cloud is absentminded is absurd.
Floating high above, traveling wherever it pleases,
It follows the bright sun, making sure to cover it.

349.

Cloud, why do you block the sun?
If you turn cumulus, this will end the severe drought.
When the north wind blows sadly, you block even the feeblest
    sunbeams.

---

[209] A traditional musical instrument, a pear-shaped five-string mandolin.

*The above poems are about blocking sunlight and hiding.*

350.

Alas, where have the days of my youth gone?
Gray hair replaced them, while I gave myself over to liquor and
 sex.
However hard I look for them, they won't return.

351.

Growing old almost in midlife is no way to be young again.
I don't want to age anymore—I want to stay as I am.
Gray hair, help me. Let me grow old slowly.

352.

No one gave it to me, nor did I receive it.
Where, then, did my enemy, Gray Hair, come from?
Gray Hair isn't fair. He makes me grow old too quickly

353.

Going gray is sad, even if I could blacken my heart after it went
 gray.
No way to blacken my hair, which turned gray earlier than
 others.
Gray Hair is never fair. He rushed at me first.


*The above poems lament growing old.*

354.

Don't laugh, boys, at the graying man.
You won't stay young either under the fair sky.
The pleasures we enjoyed when we were young seem to belong to yesterday.

355.

The hair under my ears has turned gray. People say I'm old.
My mind is young, but how can I blame them?
How very differently the young and old enjoy flowers and wine.

*The above poems are about growing old and staying young.*

356.

I'll share my grievances with the Sun and Moon.
What was so urgent in your ninety thousand li sky
That you let me age quickly, who does not loath booze and women?

357.

Who's chasing you, Golden Bird and Jade Rabbit,[210]
So that you whirl through the ninety thousand li sky?
From now on, rest every ten li.

*The above poems are about remaining alert to the passage of time.*

358.

---

[210] Refers to the sun and moon, respectively. In an old legend, a three-legged crow lives in the sun and a rabbit lives in the moon.

My friend, please don't shake the tall tree
After asking me to climb to its very top. Falling
To my death wouldn't be sad; not seeing my beloved would be
   unbearable.

359.

Did last night's wind bring this blizzard and frost?
Tall exuberant pines were nearly toppled.
What's the use of talking about flowers that never bloomed?

360.

What worm ate that tall lively tree?
Where did the long-beaked woodpecker go?
My mind sinks at the sound of falling leaves on the empty
   mountain.

*The above poems concern bruising and injuring.*

361.

Butterflies fluttering over flowers on the small hill,
Please don't light on every bough, fascinated by its fragrance.
A malicious spider, spinning its web at twilight, waits for you.

362.

The larva grew into a cicada, popped open its wings, and flew.
Its singing in the tallest tree is very good.
Please beware of the spider's web higher up in the tree.

*The above poems are about knowing when to stop.*

363.

So much rising and falling: Manwŏl Palace[211] is covered with autumn grass.
Five hundred years of royal work has turned into a cowherd's piping song.
A traveler passing at twilight cannot refrain from weeping.

364.[212]

When I ride a horse and return to the capital for five hundred years,
The mountains and rivers are the same, but the talented people are gone.
Alas, the age of peaceful happiness seems like a dream.

*The above poems are about reminiscing.*

365.[213]

---

[211] The palace of the Koryŏ dynasty.

[212] Though Kim Ch'ŏnt'aek included this sijo in the section of anonymous writers, it proved to be the work of Kil Chae (1353-1419, penname, Yaŭn), a scholar and civil servant at the end of the Koryŏ dynasty. Looking at Kaekyŏng, the dynastic capital for 500 years, Kil Chae sings of grief over his ruined country. For his refusal to serve the Chosŏn dynasty he is regarded as the epitome of loyalty, along with Chŏng Mongju and Yi Saek.

[213] One of the best known sijos in Korea, commonly called "Song of Affection," was written by Yi Chonyŏn (1269-1343), a scholar and civil official at the end of the Koryŏ dynasty.

The Milky Way points toward midnight; the moon shines on pear blossoms.
How can the cuckoo understand the spring tide set in motion by a bough?
Taken by love, as though in sickness, I can hardly sleep.

366.

Until the incense burned up in the golden censer and the water clock stopped sounding—
Where have you been and who did you devote your love to
Before returning to probe my heart, when the shadow of the moon rose?

367.

When rain scattered the pear blossoms, I parted from my beloved[214] in tears.
When the leaves fall in the autumn wind, will he think of me?
My lonely dreams wander for thousands of miles.

368.

When I die, I will become the spirit of a cuckoo.
Hidden among the inner leaves of pear-blossoming twigs,
I will cry sadly at midnight into my beloved's ear.

369.

Love is a lie—his claim to love me is a lie.

---

[214] "The beloved" in this poem refers to Yu Hŭigyŏng, a renowned poet who wrote in Chinese characters. Though he came from the lower class, he associated with many noblemen.

It's completely untrue that he saw me in a dream.
If he can't fall asleep like me, in what dream can he see me?

*The above poems are about a woman's heart.*

370.[215]

I managed to build over ten years a three-bedroom thatched house.
I'll keep one room, give one to the moon, the other to the clean wind.
No way to take in rivers and mountains—I'll enjoy them where they are.

*The above poem is about living together.*

371.

I drank until I was tipsy and fell down on a desolate mountain.
Who will wake me, when the sky and earth are my blanket and pillow?
A rough wind and drizzle woke me from my sleep.

*The above poem is about getting drunk.*

372.

---

[215] This sijo proved to be the work of Song Sun (1493-1583), a scholar and civil official of the Chosŏn dynasty. His penname was Myŏnang. After fifty years of public service, he retired to Tamyang, his home, and led a quiet life.

A friend visited me from a distant place when the vinted rice wine was gone.
The tavern is over there, but how much can you get for old clothes?
Boy, don't negotiate. Get as much as the innkeeper will give.

*The above poem is about a guest's visit.*

373.

The green glow of Mt. Samgak rose to the middle of the sky.
Paste this exuberant, auspicious aura to the palace door
And keep the old man holding a cup in nature always tipsy.

*The above poem is about a drunken hermit.*

374.

However high Mt. Tai may be, it's still a mountain under the sky.
If you climb and keep climbing, you're sure to reach the peak.
But people don't climb it—they say it's too high to climb.

*The above poem is about quitting in the middle.*

375.

Whetted for ten years, my sword is restless in its sheath.
Gazing at the mountain on the border, sometimes I touch it,
Wondering when I might do something for my country.

*The above poem is about keeping one's ambitions high.*

376.

I'll collect every sharp dagger in the world and make a broom with them
To sweep away all the barbarians of the north and south.
Then I'll make a hoe from the iron to weed the field by the river.

*The above are poems about courageously retiring.*

377.

I wish I had been born in the time of Emperor Fuxi,[216]
Even if I would have worn clothes of grass and eaten the fruit of trees.
I still miss the warm and generous minds of those people.

*The above poem is about envying the old days.*

378.

Leaning pine on the green mountain, why do you incline that way?
"Overwhelmed by a violent gale, I lie here with my roots torn asunder.
If you come across a good carpenter, please tell him I'm here."

---

[216] Refers to the peacefulness of Emperor Fuxi's reign.

*The above poem is about selling oneself.*

379.

The moon grew round and hangs in the blue sky.
With the frost and wind of many years, it's likely to fall down
But still lights the road to good wine for a drunk.

*The above poem is about getting drunk in the moonlight.*

380.

White herons, avoid the valley where the crows are fighting.
I fear they'll envy your white feathers and soil your body,
Which you diligently washed in the clear river.

*The title is missing in the original.*

381.

The sun wheels and sets as the day passes.
After fifteen nights, the moon wanes from the edge,
Like all the riches and honors in the world.

*The above poem is about waxing and waning.*

382.

Wild goose crying in flight over the northern sea at twilight,

Please carry my words to Minister Kim:[217]
Please hang on until the ram gives birth to a lamb.

*The title is missing in the original.*

383.

Failing to achieve the goals I set for myself,
After spending half my life in public service, I became a figure of ridicule.
Stop it! Why complain about living in a peaceful time?

*The above poem is about a difficult fate.*

384.

Sparrows chirp after the sun sets—
Half a twig is enough for your small bodies.
Why do you covet the whole thicket?

*The above poem is about avoiding a fight.*

385.

Even if I die, no good gravesites will be left.
Even if I have to dig myself out and swallow the elixir of life on Mt. Samsin,[218]

---

[217] Refers to Minister Sanghŏn Kim, 金尙憲, who was taken to Qing, China as a hostage after the Manchu War.
[218] 三神山: The three mountains in the sea, where hermits lived in

I'd like to be there when a new mountain rises from the sea.

*The above poem is about arriving at a distant location.*

386.

Emperor Shun's soul in Mt. Cangwu[219] followed a cloud descending on Xiaoxiang
And flew at midnight to become rain in a bamboo forest,
All to wash away the thousand-year-old tear stains of his two queens.[220]

*The above poem is about two queens.*

387.

The bright moon at the Dongting Lake[221] became the spirit
Of King Huai of Chu[222] and lit the seven hundred li flat lake
To illuminate Qu Yuan's[223] fidelity in the fish's belly.

---

Chinese legend—蓬萊山, Mt. Ponglai, 方丈山, Mt. Pangzhang, and 瀛州山, Mt Yingzhu.

[219] 倉敖山: The mountain where Emperor Shun died.

[220] Refers to two queens of Emperor Shun, Ehuang, 娥皇, and Nuying, 女英.

[221] 洞庭湖: A lake with a circumference of seven hundred li in China's Hunan Province, 湖南省.

[222] 楚懷王: The king of Chu during the Warring States period of ancient China. When he went to Qin to negotiate, he was taken hostage by King Zhao; his son, Qingxiang, became King of Chu. King Huai escaped but was recaptured and died three years later, in captivity.

[223] 屈原: A Chinese poet and politician who lived during the Warring

*The above poem is about King Huai of Chu.*

388.

Fishermen of the Zhu River, don't catch fish and boil them.
Qu Yuan's loyal heart is in the fish's belly.
It won't change, however large the pot you boil it in.

*The above poem is about Qu Yuan.*

389.

Is it possible to build a righteous nation by force?
Burning the palace of the Qin dynasty was indeed evil.
How can he evade the punishment of Heaven after killing Emperor Yi of Chu?[224]

*The above poem is about Xiang Yu.*

390.

Don't laugh at the pine tree bent by the wind.
How can flowers opening in the spring wind always be beautiful?
You'll envy me when snow flurries arrive in a light wind.

*The above poem is about a pine tree.*

---

States period. When his advice was ignored, he drowned himself in the Miulo River (汨羅水) and became food for fish.

[224] 義帝, King Huai of Chu, see note 219.

391.

Who says the snow-bent bamboos are crooked?
If their fidelity is bendable, how do they stay green in the snow?
Perhaps they're the only ones who keep faith even in the cold.

*The above poem is about bamboo.*

392.

The empty mountain is desolate and the cuckoo cries sadly.
The rise and fall of the Shu dynasty is not a thing of today or yesterday.
But why does your cry slice through my bowels?

*The above poem is about a cuckoo.*

393.

Peaceful reign like this, peaceful reign like that.
The time of Emperor Yao and the time of Emperor Shun.
We all want to enjoy the time of this peaceful reign.

*The above poem is about a peaceful reign.*

394.

Mind, why are you always young?
When I'm old, why don't you grow old?
I'm afraid people will laugh at me, when I chase you.

*The above poem is about guarding one's mind.*

395.

If my past had been like that, nothing would remain of my features.
My worries turned into threads tied up here and there.
There's no end to it, however hard I try to untangle them.

*The above poem is about hard work.*

396.

Until Mt. Tai becomes a flat field and the sea turns to land,
I'll carry out my filial duty to my parents living in the northern house.
I'll become Jiqi[225] in the peaceful reign, with no time to grow old.

*The above poem is about filial duty.*

397.

Flowers opened in the night rain, and vinted rice wine ripened.
My friend is supposed to come with the moon, bringing his geomungo.
Boy, the moon is on the eaves. See if my guest has arrived.

---

[225] 稷契: Ji was the Yu dynasty official in charge of agriculture and Qi was the Yu dynasty official in charge of water management.

*The above poem is about waiting for guests.*

**Samsaktaeyŏp,** 三數大葉: A lyric tune representative of the eighteenth century, faster than yisaktaeyŏp.

398.

Because vassals should die for the king, I deserve death.
The reason I'm still alive, wearing a long sword,
Is to witness our benevolent king's great virtues revive again.

399.

Honors are proof of disgrace, riches bring toil and trouble.
Becoming an old fisherman on the boundless expanse of the sea,
I'll come and go when the bright sun shines on the water.

400.

When flowers fall and leaves bud, the shade surges.
I snap pine boughs to sweep away the cattails.
The sound of an oriole wakes me from a drunken sleep.

401.

Planted bamboos made a fence and cultivated pines became a pavilion.
Who will know I'm in a place covered by white clouds?
A crane circles the garden. I think it's my friend.

402.

Nothing to do in a thatched house, I lay my head on my
    geomungo,
Hoping to find in dream a peaceful reign.
But a fisherman's piping wakes me from sleep.

403.

The light wind that melted snow on the green mountain is gone.
I'd like to borrow it for a moment to waft over my head
And melt the old frost under my ears.

404.

Ah, I was deceived. The fall moon and spring wind cheated on
    me.
I believed in them, because they never failed to arrive in every
    season
But they followed the young boy, leaving the gray hair all to me.

405.

Life is pitiable, like weeds floating on water.
We found each other by accident and parted in a flash.
If we later meet again, I think it was preordained.

406.

People of the world, you think you have two lives—
Just keep saving, not knowing how to eat and enjoy things.
What will become of your houseful of gold and jade after you
    die?

407.

Don't say this or that is so, passing on the news of the world.
I have no interest in other people's disputes.
If my wine ripens in an earthen jar, that's good enough for me.

408.

Don't say this or that is right—let's just drink and play.
If you get tipsy, go to sleep.
I'd like to forget the worries while I'm drunk and asleep.

409.

When I drunkenly stagger about, I swear off drinking.
But when I hold a cup and look at the wine, my vow is futile.
What's the use of talking about a drunken vow?

410.

Ah, when I die, please bury me in the east hill of the jar maker's house.
I want to become a jug when my white bones turn to dust
In which to distil the liquor I never drank enough of when I was alive.

411.

All the peach blossoms in the garden fell in last night's wind.
A boy holds a broom and tries to sweep them away.
The fallen blossoms are still blossoms—why not leave them alone?

412.

Did the wind from a couple of days ago ruffle the rivers and

lakes?
How are the fishermen by the river doing anyway?
Living for a long time in the mountains, I have no news of them.

413.

The open sea looks at jumping fish and the boundless sky lets birds fly.
Born a man, how can I not know high spirits?
It won't do any harm to be kind to people and help them.

414.

Pity, alas, the world! Why is it so busy?
When did the pentachord stop at Namhun Palace?
I'm sad about the rainstorms blowing dizzily over this time.

415.

On a breezy day, the phoenix comes to dance
And peach and apricot blossoms fall in the fortress.
What blossoms will the bent pine tree in the mountain shed?

416.

Birds come back to sleep and the new moon rises.
A Buddhist monk crossing the single log bridge alone—
How far is your temple, where the bell rings in the distance?

417.

On a day of wind mixed with frost, I filled a gold pot
With just-opened yellow chrysanthemums and sent it to the

Office of Special Advisers.
Peach and plum blossoms, don't pretend to be flowers. I know my beloved's will.

418.

White herons, don't laugh at crows, saying they're black.
What's black on the outside isn't necessarily black on the inside.
You may be the only ones who are white on the outside and black inside.

419.

Meishan Pavilion[226] is desolate. Only the grass is green.
Tianshou Tomb[227] is empty. Only a white cloud sinks.
I'm so sad about the rise and fall of this old nation.

420.

People of the world talk too much.
They find fault with others, while ignoring their own.
Don't find another's faults. Correct your own.

421.

A real drinker doesn't care if the wine is good or bad. Sweet or bitter.
I'll filter it to drink my fill from my own cup or offer cups to

---

[226] 煤山閣: A pavilion in Meishan, a royal court in the Xicheng District, Beijing, also called Jingshan. Chongzhen, the last emperor of the Ming dynasty, committed suicide there.
[227] 天壽陵: The thirteen tombs of the Ming dynasty emperors in Changping District, Beijing.

others.
So what if I lie down in a stupor, in a thatched house under the bright moon.

422.

Gloriously drunk at twilight, I was carried off on the back of a donkey
And travelled ten li in the mountains and rivers of a dream.
The piping of a fisherman woke me from that sleep.

423.

Holding the rein, petitioning in vain, they couldn't die in the Yin dynasty.[228]
In what land did the ferns on Mt. Shuyang grow?
How could they eat them, though they were merely wild grass?

424.

Lord Zhou was a saint. People of the world, please listen to me.
This son of King Wen and brother of King Wu
Betrayed no hint of arrogance in his life.

425.

---

[228] Boyi and Shuqi held the reins of Zhou Emperor Wu's horse, imploring him not to attack the tyrant Zhou of Yin. But he ignored them and destroyed the Yin dynasty. Refusing to eat grain produced in the Zhou dynasty, they retired to Mt. Shuyang, where they starved to death.

"Nan Ba, a man should die rather than surrender."[229]
He laughed, saying, "Because my lord says so, I will dare to die."
How many tears will our weeping heroes shed?

426.

Who can compete with Lord Xinling[230] in wealth and luxury?
But it won't take a hundred years for a plow to pass over his grave.
So what's the use of talking about common people?

427.

When I come out, shouldering a jar of wine vinted two days ago,
The boys in the house laugh and shout.
I want to bid adieu to the passing of spring in the rivers and lakes.

428.

I want the warm sunlight of winter to shine on my beloved
And offer him bunches of spring water parsley to taste.
He doesn't need anything, but I can't forget him.

429.

---

[229] 南八, Nan Ba: 南霽雲, Nan Juyun in the Tang dynasty. 張巡 Zhang Zun said this to Nan Ba, when they were captured during the An Lushan Rebellion. He is the lord in the second line.

[230] 信陵君 was a prominent aristocrat, statesman, and general, one of the Four Lords of the Warring States. He had three thousand house guests as retainers in his service.

Ah, people of the world, we cannot always do the right thing.
We do the wrong thing, deliberately, and fall into unnecessary disgrace.
Knowing this, we should do the right thing.

430.

If gray hair represented rank and fame, people would compete with each other
And no one like me could gain that even in old age.
But gray hair is the fairest and most just thing in the world.

431.

Do I know the things of the world? I'll go to the bank of the Wei River,
Since my friends hate me. Does nature also hate me?
I'll become a fisherman and wait in nature for good luck.

432.

If I'm sincere in word and deed, and trustworthy, and do no wrong,
I'll come to no harm, and no one will hate me.
I'll practice this and commit myself to study, if I have any spare time.

433.

I pull on the boughs of red jujubes to pick the fruit
And strike the early chestnut boughs with ripened nuts.
The wine is overflowing when my friends and I enter the thatched house.

434.

Because people mistake wrong for right and right for wrong,
I don't know what's happening to them out in the world.
I'd rather act as if I was wrong and they were right.

435.

Anxiety and joy are evenly divided, even if you live to a hundred.
And since there's no guarantee you'll live to a hundred,
I'll drink and play around until I reach that age.

436.

Peach, pear, and apricot blossoms, all fragrant grasses, don't resent the spring sun.
You go on endlessly with the creation of the world.
I'm sad we have at best only a hundred years.

437.

Even great-spirited Ba Wang of Chu[231] hated separation more than death,
Shedding tears at the sad song sung in his consort's tent.[232]
But I heard no words in his weeping at the wind and waves of the Wu River.

---

[231] Refers to 項羽, Xiang Yu, who destroyed the Qin dynasty and founded the Western Chu dynasty. Defeated in battle by 劉邦, Liu Bang, the founding emperor of the Han dynasty, he committed suicide on the bank of the Wu River, 烏江.

[232] Trapped by Liu Bang's forces at Gaixia, 垓下, Xiang Yu wrote a song to sing with his weeping consort Yu, 虞美人.

438.

Whether my death is violent or peaceful will make no difference once I'm gone.
I won't know whether someone plows a field or weeds the rice paddy above my grave.
Since wine cannot penetrate the dirt in Liu Ling's[233] grave, what can I do but play?

439.

Don't gossip about others, saying you like to talk.
If you talk about others, they'll talk about you.
Talk inspires more talk. Thus it's good not to talk.

440.

Once gone, he never appears even in dream, as if he has forgotten me.
No way! How could he forget me?
My longing is what makes me blame only him.

441.

Weak and splendid is the goose in the autumn sky!
My beloved should have known that when you appeared.
You only honk and pass by—he didn't tie a note around you.

---

[233] 劉伶, (221-300CE), was a Chinese poet and scholar notorious for his love of alcohol. One of the Seven Sages of the Bamboo Grove, Liu Ling was a Taoist who retreated to the countryside to pursue a spontaneous, natural existence, which would have been impossible under the tight constraints of the imperial court.

442.

It's not true the November night is long.
On the day of my beloved's visit even the sky hates me.
It wakes the cock early to crow and ushers my beloved out.

443.

The moon reflected on the snow fills the window. Wind, don't blow.
Of course I know this isn't the sound of his dragging shoes,
But I think it may be him, when I feel lonely and miss him.

444.

The candlelight outside my window—from whom have you parted
In tears, unaware that you're burning out?
Like the candle, we unwittingly burn ourselves out.

445.

I see the distant mountain turn white with snow.
It will turn green when the snow melts.
But my hair will never go back to black once it turns white.

446.

Great roc, don't laugh at the tiny wren.
Like you, it flies in the boundless sky.
What difference is there between you two birds?

447.

Before Fan Li,[234] Minister of Yue, acquired a name and wealth,
He knew the pleasures of enjoying the moonshine on a boat in Taihu[235]
And returned late, saying he would win the hand of Xi Shi.

448.

When I say no more wine, the glass fills by itself.
Who's in the wrong, me drinking the wine or the wine filling my glass?
Holding a cup, I ask the moon who's to blame.

449.

The heaven and earth of Yao and Shun, the sun and moon of Yao and Shun.
Heaven and earth, sun and moon—the same for Yao and Shun as from antiquity.
I don't know why the things of the world change day by day.

450.

On a horse moving like a dragon, with a falcon taller than one cha,
I head up the mountain trail with my dog at twilight.
Nothing better for a man's amusement.

451.

---

[234] 范蠡: An ancient Chinese military strategist, politician, and businessman. He retired from public service to live in seclusion with his wife Xu Shi, a famous beauty in Chinese history.
[235] 太湖, Taihu, in the Yangtze delta, also known as Lake Tai or Lake Taihu, is one of China's largest freshwater lakes.

After fifty years in power, I still don't know the things of the world.
I try to listen to the wishes of the people.
Hearing children sing in the bustling street, I assume all is well.

452.

On a bright moonlit night in Nanxun Hall,[236] with eight good and eight gentle souls,[237]
The music of the five-string lyre resolved my people's resentment.
We, too, will enjoy a peaceful reign under our benevolent king.

**Naksijo** 樂時調: A sijo tune considered to be endlessly pleasing, like a flower garden on a sunny day, published in a mid-eighteenth-century anthology.

453.

I lost my fishing rod when I nodded off, and my straw raincoat when I was dancing.
White seagulls, don't laugh at an old man's senility.
I can hardly bear the springtide of the ten li peach blossoms over there.

454.

A galloping horse stops when I say "owang," and an ox moves

---

[236] 南薰殿: The palace in which Emperor Shun played a five-string lyre to sing of the southern wind.
[237] Refers to the eight sons of Gao Shin, 高申, and the eight sons of Gao Yang, 高陽.

at "t'a."
Even a cruel tiger will turn around, once I teach it how.
But what kind of woman is my wife, who never listens to my instructions?

455.

A shadow falls on the water, and I see a monk passing by.
Please stop. I need to know where you're going.
Pointing to a white cloud, he continues on his way wordlessly.

456.

It's really good to see a lonely bamboo on a rock edge.
A lonely bamboo—who is "Guzhu Jun"[238] to you?
It seems I saw Boyi and Shuqi in the clean wind of Mt. Shuyang.

457.

Love, love, a long love, a love like a stream.
Though it scatters in a boundless sky, it still overflows.
The love of my beloved seems endless.

458.

No trace will remain on the fine sand under the sea, however hard I tread on it.
Nor will I know what's in my beloved however he may love me.
Like a boatman who shakes in a strong gust, I don't know the depths of my love.

---

[238] 孤竹君: Refers to Ya Wei, father of Boyi and Shuqi and ruler of Ghuzu State.

459.

How was love? Was it round or broad?
Long or short? One pal²³⁹ or one cha?²⁴⁰
It didn't last long, but it could slice up my bowels.

460.

Today is a good day, this place is a good place.
Good people are gathered in a good place, on a good day.
Good wines, good side dishes—it's good to play.

461.

When rain falls around ch'ŏngmyŏng,²⁴¹ I hang banknotes around the donkey's neck
And say to the cowherds, "Where's the tavern?"
"Ask over there, where the apricot blossoms fall."

462.

Green mountains exist by themselves, green waters by themselves,
Mountains by themselves, water by itself, and me among them by myself.
Alas, my body grew old all by itself.

---

²³⁹ A traditional unit of length, roughly six feet or the arm span of a man.
²⁴⁰ A traditional unit of length, 30.3 cm.
²⁴¹ One of the twenty-four divisions of the year on the lunar calendar, around April 5th.

**Changjinjusa**: A Song to Offer Wine written by Chŏng Ch'ŏl (1536-1593). It is the title and tune of the song.

463.

Let's drink a cup, then another, let's drink many cups, marking the number with snapped flower boughs. It doesn't matter if in death I'll be covered with a straw mat and tied to a chige[242] or carried off in a magnificent bier, followed by a crowd of weeping mourners. Once I enter the forest of silver grasses, scouring rushes, oaks, and white poplars, who will ask me to drink with them when the yellow sun, white moon, fine rain, large flakes of snow, and a lonely wind blow? What use is regret when monkeys whistle over my grave?

The above "Changjinjusa" was written by Songang,[243] in imitation of Li Bai and Li He[244] and borrowing Du Fu's phrase, "There's a procession of many people in mourning dress. See how the man goes, his body tightly bound." The meaning of the lyric is conveyed thoroughly and the words are sad and remorseful. If Meng Changjun hears this song, it will not be only Yongmen's geomungo[245] that will shed tears.

---

[242] A frame-shaped transport rack.
[243] Penname of Chŏng Ch'ŏl (鄭澈 1536-1593), who wrote dozens of sijos, including "Songs of Teaching People" and four prose poems, among them, "Hymn of Constancy."
[244] 李賀, Li He, a mid-Tang dynasty Chinese poet, whose courtesy name was Changji. He wrote *JiangJinjiu*, 將進酒.
[245] 雍門琴: Refers to Yongmen's instrument and the tune. He made people laugh and cry with his geomungo. When he played for Meng Changjun a geomungo song whose theme was the evanescence of fame and riches in the world, Meng was said to have wept.

**Song of Meng Changjun**[246]: A song by an anonymous writer. It is the title and tune of the song.

464.

Who was more glorious than Meng Changjun a thousand years ago? And who is sadder than him now? Did he have few houseguests? Did he lack fame? His life was saved with the help of a dog, a thief, a cock, and some people. His hair turned gray, he died, thorns grew on his grave. Did he ever think that cowherds and boys carrying wood would walk over his grave singing sad songs? Meng Changjun's sighing seems to rise up and down to the geomungo tune of Yongmen Zhou.[247] Boy, tune the geomungo. I'll play it while I'm still alive.

The above "Song of Meng Changjun" was written by an anonymous poet, who believed the glory of the world was but a daydream and posthumous glory inferior to the pleasures of the world. If Meng Changjun's soul hears this, his tears will surely wet his collar in the next world.

Because the songs of our countrymen were written mainly in Korean, with Chinese characters occasionally inserted, they were passed down in Korean books. They couldn't help but use Korean, which was the custom of the country, and while their songs do not compare to Chinese songs, some are worth

---

[246] Refers to 田文, Tian Wen, an aristocratic statesman in the Qi Kingdom and one of the Four Lords of the Warring States period; remembered for saving his own life on a visit to Qin, with the help of a thief who was once his houseguest and a man who could mimic the cock's crow.
[247] A geomungo master in the Ji dynasty during the Warring States period. It is said his playing made Meng Changjun cry.

listening to. The so-called Chinese songs are ancient ballads, with new music, sung to wind and string instruments. When we use Korean, we have to adjust them to the Chinese characters. Ours are different from Chinese songs, but they express the minds of our writers, their melodies are harmonious, and since they prompt us to recite them, licentiously indulging ourselves, moving our hands and feet to dance, they are no different.

    I have selected the most popular ones to write down.

**Manhoengch'ŏngnyu** 蔓橫清類: It is a collection of tunes called manhoeng and songs with similar tunes. Manhoeng is the sound of singing songs cunningly. Ch'ŏng means the sound of singing a high note. This is music in the tradition of nong, nak, and p'yŏn, and is used to sing songs with many lyrics.

Manhoengch'ŏngnyu's lyrics are obscene and trivial and cannot serve as a model to follow. But they have a long history, which cannot be discarded, so I wrote them down below.

465.

Walking along Mt. Kaegol in Kwangwon-do, I can catch the
    white peregrine perched atop a tall fir tree behind the
    Yujŏm Temple,
Tame it, and then release it for the pheasant hunt.
But as for my new love? I have no idea how to tame her.

466.

Though we can get a half-sheaf of sorghum straw from
    Kŭmsŏng, Kimhwa, build a hut the size of a bushel,
And dip white poplar chopsticks into millet porridge or non-

glutinous rice soup to offer each other, saying I don't like it, I don't want to know the world of separation for as long as I live.

467.

Did you watch the carriage pass, carrying people's lives?
I've seen how fast eighty years passed over the hill of seventy.
It passed, but I've never stopped talking about the pleasures of youth.

468.

The heart of a man leaving his love behind, and the heart of a man left behind—
The former's horse cannot go forward thanks to the snow heaped on Namjŏnkwan.[248]
Fragrant grasses return every year, but another's grudge never ends.

469.

It rained yesterday on Dongshan, and I played Go with old Xie An.[249]
This moonlit night, with Li Bai in a thatched house and a hundred poems on a mal of wine.

---

[248] 藍田關, Lantianguan: Lantian Pass, the gateway to the ancient capital of Chang'an, southeast of Xianyang, was a battleground for military strategists in every dynasty. The phrase alludes to Han Yu's poem.
[249] The courtesy name of Anshi, formally Duke Wenjing of Luling, a Jin dynasty statesman who, despite his lack of military experience, saved the dynasty from attacks by former Qin.

Tomorrow, a big party downtown with Du Fu and ladies of Handan.[250]

470.

How did Li Bai drink three hundred cups of wine a day?
What was it about Du Mu[251] that prompted people to fill his carriage with oranges when he passed, drunkenly, through Yangzhou?[252]
I really envy the demeanor of those two.

471.

Xiang Yu was the strongest man, but he shed tears when he left Consort Yu.
Emperor Tang Minghuang[253] saved the world, but he wept on leaving Yang Guifei.[254]
What use is there in talking about a dozen other men?

472.

When a gold toad shaman performed the chin'ogwisaenam

---

[250] The capital of the Zhao dynasty, renowned for its songs, dances, and beautiful women.
[251] Du Mu was a leading Chinese poet of the late Tang dynasty. His courtesy name was Muzhi, and he is best known for his lyrical and romantic quatrains.
[252] When he passed, drunkenly, through Yangzhu, women filled his cart with oranges.
[253] Emperor Xuanzong of Tang, commonly known as Emperor Ming of Tang.
[254] Yang Yuhuan, also known as Yang Guifei, was the beloved consort of Emperor Xuanzong of Tang in his later years; one of the Four Beauties of ancient China.

ritual[255] the night a green frog died of a stomach ache,
A green grasshopper musician played changgu[256] tum-tum and a black grasshopper piper trilled on a horizontal bamboo flute.
Somewhere a crawfish carrying a stone banged on a drum.

473.

A man has nothing to do in the world!
I want to be literate, but literacy begets anxiety. I want to brandish a sword, but the mastery of martial arts is a deadly weapon.
Thus I'd rather go back and forth between the party quarter and the taverns.

474.

Noblewomen of the world, please don't laugh at this poor scholar.
For all his wealth Shi Chong[257] ended up an ordinary man, while poor Yan Hui[258] became a saint.
Poor as I am, I don't envy the wealth of others while I pursue my own way.

475.

My love went aimlessly out one night when the moon had set.
Where is he wandering, riding a white horse with a golden whip?
    Hooked on booze and women, did he forget to return?

---

[255] A shamanistic ritual to lead the soul of a dead man to Heaven.
[256] Hourglass-shaped double-headed drum.
[257] A Western Jin dynasty statesman who led a luxurious life.
[258] Confucius's favorite disciple, venerated in Confucian temples as one of the Four Sages.

When tears fall like rain, overcome by longing in my solitude,
  I toss and turn, I can't sleep.

476.

Ah, I dipped a yellow weasel brush into Suyangmaewŏl[259] ink
And put it on the windowsill. But it rolled off and vanished. If
  I walk around,
I may find it. Anyone who tries it out will know its worth.

477.

Who seized my beloved, keeping him from coming home until
  dew settles on the pear blossoms?
When one says, "Don't go," tugging at his clothes, it will be
  difficult for him to break free for no apparent reason.
Oh my beloved, look into your heart. Are you so different from
  him?

478.

What can I do? What should I do? My mother-in-law, what can
  I do?
I broke the bronze paddle scooping rice for my lover. What
  can I do, my mother-in-law?
My daughter-in-law, don't worry. When I was young, I broke it
  many times.

479.

Will the nightjar fly into the sky? Will the mole enter the earth?
A golden skylark caught in the wire net flaps its wings. Can it

---

[259] A high-quality ink stick from Haeju, Hwanghae Province.

fly? Crawl? Where can it go?
I'd like to flap my wings, too, now that I have a new lover.

480.

How can I touch that woman's jade-like breasts?
I want to caress them, like the turned-in collar of a silk chŏksam[260] under a purple toju silk[261] chakchŏgori.[262]
When my sweaty hands stick to her breasts, I forget how to remove them.

481.

Three monks walking along the bending road under the pine tree.
I ask the last one, "Where does the Buddha sit, the one who taught separation from the human world and a solitary life?"
"This poor monk does not know, but my sister priest knows."

482.

Clean wind and the bright moon. A wise man likes water, a virtuous man likes mountains, and benevolent noblemen wear black bandanas[263] on their white heads.

---

[260] A Korean-style unlined summer jacket.
[261] Yellow thick silk.
[262] Refers to an outer jacket and inner jacket worn together. Korean woman used to wear an inner jacket on top of a chŏksam and an outer jacket over them.
[263] The headdress worn with official attire.

An old man of Shino[264] and an old man of Langya[265] were reborn in our country and sang a Zizhi Qu[266]—there is no pleasure like living beyond the secular world.
I pray to help our good wise king rule the nation well, and bring peace to the people.

483.

White clouds spread over ten thousand li and moonlight shines on the front and back streams.
An old man stops fishing, skewers his catch, and crosses the collapsed bridge. Gazing at the apricot blossoms, he shuffles into the tavern.
His taste is the most exalted! I suppose its worth cannot be calculated in cash.

484.

When I circled the deep mountain three or four times,
A heavy frost fell here and there and a light snow was sprinkled on the thin ice right after noon in May. You should have seen it.
My love, my love, figure things out for yourself, despite what others say.

485.

---

[264] Refers to Yi Yin, an honored minister in the early Shang dynasty, who helped Tang, the founder of the Shang dynasty, defeat King Jie of Xia.
[265] Refers to Zhuge Kiang, a Chinese politician, military strategist, writer, engineer, and inventor, who served as chancellor and regent of Shu Han during the Three Kingdoms period.
[266] A song about the pleasures of rural life, written by the Four Figures of Shangshan.

The sun, moon, and stars are those of the Heavenly Sovereign,[267] the sun, moon, stars, mountains, streams, and lands are those of the Earthly Sovereign.
Though the sun, moon, stars, mountains, streams, and lands are the same ones in the time of the Heavenly Sovereign and the Earthly Sovereign,
Why are there no people in the time of the Human Sovereign?

486.

If you know you'll live for a hundred years, will you refrain from wine and women?
It will be very sad if you don't live to a hundred, even if you've restrained yourself.
One's life is ordained by Heaven and living to a hundred isn't easy, even if you restrain yourself.

487.

Alas, Ba Wang of Chu.[268] It's really sad!
If, blessed with the power to extract a mountain from the earth and the spirit to overthrow the world, you had practiced benevolence and righteousness, sparing Emperor Yi,[269]
You would not have been so helpless, even if there were ten

---

[267] The Heavenly Sovereign 天皇氏 was the first legendary Chinese king after Pangu's era. He was one of the Three Sovereigns along with the Earthly Sovereign 地皇氏 and Human Sovereign 人皇氏.
[268] Refers to Xiang Yu, a noble and warlord in Chu, who rebelled against the Qin dynasty. He was granted the title of Duke of Lu by King Huai II for restoring the Chu state in 208 BC.
[269] Refers to Emperor Yi of Chu, also known as King Huai II of Chu, who ruled Chu in the late Qin dynasty. He was killed by Xiang Yu.

Pei Gong.[270]

488.

What is it about the mountains and rivers of Beimang[271] that everyone cannot help but go there?
Both Qin Shi Huang[272] and Han Wudi[273] tried to avoid it, seeking an elixir of life.
Alas, I feel sad in the wind and rain of Lishan,[274] the pines and nut pines of Wuling.

489.

Who said you can forget your worries when you're dead drunk?
When I miss beauty from a corner under the sky, even a hundred cups don't help.
The thought of my graying mother leaning on the door, waiting for me, makes me sadder yet.

490.

I wish I was younger—fifteen years younger.

---

[270] Refers to Liu Bang, Emperor Gaozu of Han, founder and first emperor of the Han dynasty.
[271] A mountain in Luoyang, where there are said to be many graves; a symbol of a graveyard.
[272] The founder of the Qin dynasty and the first emperor of a unified China. From 247 to 221 BC, he was Zheng, King of Qin, until the Qin conquered all the other Warring States.
[273] Refers to Emperor Wu of Han, formally enshrined as Emperor Wu the Filial; born Liu Che, courtesy name Tong, he was the seventh emperor of the Han dynasty in ancient China.
[274] The mountain in which the tomb of Emperor Qin Shihuang is located.

My beautiful face is hollow as a weeping willow stump by a stream.
The pleasures of my youth seem like it was just yesterday.

491.

If I could buy medicine to cure illnesses born of drinking
And medicine to live a long life, though I enjoy sex, I wouldn't mind the cost.
But since I can't buy them, I'll restrain myself a little to live to a hundred.

492.

At a silk window, in a white wall at midnight, I meet a woman beautiful enough to cause the downfall of a country.
Under a jade-green silk blanket, face to face on amber pillows, we enjoy ourselves, like a pair of mandarin ducks playing affectionately, cleaving the green water.
Why should I envy King Qingxiang of Chu[275] for meeting a celestial maiden in Wushan?[276]

493.

My dog barks at the twig gate and I go out, thinking it's my beloved.
My love isn't there, only moonlight filling the garden. It was the sound of leaves falling in a gust of autumn wind.
My dog, why do you deceive me barking at the leaves falling in

---

[275] King Qingxiang ruled the state of Chu from 298 to 263 BC, during the Warring States period.
[276] Legend has it that King Qingxing met a celestial maiden in Wushan and made love to her.

the autumn wind?

494.

A maiden who looked in vain for her husband turned into a ghost after death.
"I'll become Indian mallow in the hemp field to use as a diaper for a toothless old monk in the Kaegol Temple on Mt. Yongmun.
When he sweats and itches, I'll rub him gently."

495.

The peregrine high in the blue sky considers a thousand square miles nothing.
But the duck pecking in the ditch for food thinks
It must be ten thousand li across the threshold of its house.

496.

Wild goose, solitary wild goose flying your own way,
Please stop by the Seoul fortress and shout one thing over and over:
"I'm hurrying on my own way, and I don't know if I'll make it."

497.

With Emperor Han Wu's conquest of the northern and western barbarians, Zhuge Liang's seven captives and seven releases,[277]
And Governor-General Xie's majesty on Mt. Bagong, I'll

---

[277] Zhuge Liang 諸葛亮 captured and released Meng Zheng 孟獲 seven times, securing his final surrender.

sweep away barbarians everywhere,
Destroy the palace in Mongolia, and report on my success,
singing a song of triumph.

498.

The water flowing through Yangdŏk, Maengsan, Ch'ŏlsan, and Kasan goes under Pubyŏk Pavilion,
The water flowing through Mahŭraki, Kongiso, Tumi, and Wŏlkye goes under Chech'ŏn Pavilion.
The tears I shed, longing for my beloved, go under my pillow.

499.

When Emperor Taizu of Song entered the sea, the waters of which whales drank up and gushed out in the attack on Jinling,[278]
He built a bridge, as if to carve out a rainbow with Cao Bin's[279] sharp knife.
If my love crosses over that bridge, I'll hurry over it.

500.

Sima Qian's immortal writing, Wang Xizhi's calligraphy that cowers a thousand men,
Liu Ling's enjoyment of wine, and Du Mu's ardor—you can possess these if you pursue them throughout your life.
But it's difficult to possess Emperor Shun and Zengzi's filial duty, Long Pang and Bi Gan's fidelity.

---

[278] Old name for Nanjing.
[279] A famous military general of the Song dynasty.

501.

A tiny needle and a mid-sized needle fell into the wide sea.
It's said that a dozen boatmen tied the dull ends of their poles and threaded the needles, shouting all at once.
My love, my love, figure things out for yourself, despite what others say.

502.

The blue silk curtain window wavered and I went out, thinking my love had come.
He wasn't there, only moonlight in the garden. It was the shadow of a phoenix that landed on the wet leaves of a sultan's parasol, trimming its feathers.
Whoops, I'm lucky it was night. Otherwise, I would have been a laughing stock.

503.

No matter how much I urge the black ox eating leaves in the bean field to go away, crying "irya," where can it go?
No matter how much I urge my love under the blanket to leave, kicking and pushing him away, where can he go, leaving me alone?
My love, I think, is the only one I fight who will never break away.

504.

Carrying broken arrows, a snapped gun, and a soldered small brass kettle, I reproach the Yellow Emperor.[280]

---

[280] The Yellow Emperor, whose name was Huangdi, one of the

Before people stole from one other, they were generous, the world was peaceful, and they lived for eighteen thousand years.[281]
Alas, why did they torment their descendants, teaching them to use spears and shields?

505.

How harsh will the autumn rains be? Don't take out your raingear and chingnyŏng.[282]
How far can we get on our trip of ten li? Don't strike the limping donkey with a whip to speed it up with its bad back and stomachache.
I'd like to take a break, if I come across a tavern.

506.

Evening approaches. Once day is done, it will dawn again—and then my love will leave.
I won't see him after that. If I can't see him, I'll miss him. Then I'll take sick, which will mean my death.
If you know I'll take sick and die, can you stay over tonight before you leave?

507.

A gray-haired harlot wanted a young husband.
She dyed her hair black and, crossing a high rugged mountain

---

legendary Chinese sovereigns and cultural heroes. He is said to have invented weapons, ships, and carts.
[281] The Yellow Emperor is said to have lived for eighteen thousand years.
[282] A coat with a straightened collar.

pass, ran into an unexpected rain shower, which turned her
white jacket collar black and her hair gray.
She's ruined. Almost no chance of that crone's wish being
granted.

508.

I lost my virginity at forty, confused, flustered, desperate.
I entered her this way and that. My old bachelor's heart was
exhilarated.
Had I known this pleasure before, I would have done it from
when I began to crawl.

509.

Though the ancients warned us to refrain from boozing and
womanizing,
It's hard not to get drunk when the jar of fragrant wine is full
and I recite poems with my friends on tapchŏngjŏl[283] and
tŭnggojŏl.[284]
I can't help sleeping with a beauty when I can't sleep alone by
a lonely lamplight in an inn.

510.

Emperor Shun's lyre at Nanxun Hall[285] was handed down to
the Xia, Yin, and Zhou dynasties.
But royal statesmanship faded and proper music ceased amid

---

[283] March 3rd (lunar calendar), when people used to go to the fields to walk on the new grass.
[284] September 9th (lunar calendar), when people used to climb mountains to enjoy wine and food.
[285] The place where Emperor Shun lived.

the fight for superiority in the Qin, Han, and Tang dynasties
and the warfare of the Song, Qi, and Liang dynasties.
A sage was born in our country to continue playing the lyre
and singing the Nanfeng poem.

511.

The tall pine over the hill sways when the wind blows.
For what does the willow by the stream swing?
It's natural to weep in longing for my love, but why do I
whimper and sniffle?

512.

A Buddhist monk grabs a Buddhist nun's hair, and she grabs
his hair knot.
Their hair entangled, they wrangle with each other over who's
right,
Watched over by blind men, while a deaf mute somewhere says
who's right, who's wrong.

513.

This age of our king and parents is peaceful.
Thanks to our king's virtue, an auspicious wind and clouds
come. Thanks to the blessings of my parents, we don't
worry about food and firewood.
Everyone is excited about the harvest, enjoying the wine and
chicken.

514.

I cut up my long robe of a Buddhist monk to make unlined
trousers and a summer jacket, then untied my prayer beads

to make a crupper for the donkey.
The words of Amida world, Avalokiteśvara, Namo Amitabha Buddha, ten years of studying[286]—I gladly cast them away.
I enter into a woman Buddhist's breasts at midnight, I have no time for prayer.

515.

How can a serious illness caused by longing for my beloved be cured?
If I ask a doctor for medicine, or let a blind man perform an exorcism, or call a shaman to pray while scratching the willow basket, will I be cured?
I sincerely believe I would get better immediately if my beloved were with me.

516.

Let's play now and always. Let's play day and night.
Let's play until the yellow cock painted on the wall flutters its wings and cranes its neck to crow many times.
Our life is but morning dew—how can we refrain from playing?

517.

That man in white clothes over there is really quick and gallant.
He crosses the small stone bridge and then the big stone bridge, running quickly, horizontally. Oh, dear, I'd like to take him as my husband.
If he can't be my husband, I wish he would be my friend's husband.

---

[286] The words of a Buddhist chant.

518.

Her eyebrows are like a male butterfly landing, her teeth like lined gourd seeds.
She smiles at me like three-colored peach blossoms opening halfway at the touch of rain.
When your parents begot you, they wanted you to love only me.

519.

When I hug her tightly, I feel her slender, limber waist.
When I lift up her red skirt, I see her shapely snow-white skin. And when I lift my legs to straddle her, a blossoming red peony opens in the spring wind.
Coming in and in, going out and out—the sound of a water mill on a thickly forested mountain.

520.

When a toad with a fly in its mouth rushed to alight on a dung heap
And gaze at the distant mountain, it saw a peregrine in flight, and its heart sank. Down it jumped to hide, pitching into the dung.
"Whoops! I'm lucky to be so agile. Otherwise, I would have bruised myself."

521.

In the small legendary land of Wu Huai,[287] under the sky in

---

[287] An ancient emperor in Chinese legend who established rules for an ideal society.

Fuxi, I carefully selected a spot to build a small thatched cottage.
The cloud-covered mountain, blue-misted river, wind blowing through pine trees, moonlight shining through vines, wild animals, mountain birds, all became mine, naturally.
Boy, I'm afraid that others might steal the wealth of this old man on the mountain.

522.

I was dead drunk last night and dreamed of drunkenness.
Holding a long sword, I rode a swift horse across the distant sea. After conquering the Huns, I returned to the palace and briefed the king about my successful campaign.
My manly righteous spirit is so heavy I'm testing it in dreams.

523.

Who from antiquity lived wisely enough for history to remember them?
Fan Li's [288] retreat to Wuhu, Zhang Liang's [289] attempt to become a hermit, Shu Guang [290] squandering his fortune, Ji Ying [291] returning home in the autumn wind, and Tao Yuanming in rural seclusion.
Next to them, what use is there in counting all the corrupt officials?

---

[288] See note 152.
[289] A strategist and statesman who lived in the early Western Han dynasty, known as one of the "Three Heroes of the early Han dynasty."
[290] A Confucian scholar and official in the late Former Han period.
[291] Zhang Han's other name, a high official in the Jin dynasty.

524.

Chasu[292] Yi rides an ox, Yakchŏng[293] Kim carries a barrel-shaped earthen jar,
Kwŏnnong[294] Nam and tangjang[295] Cho stagger drunkenly, dancing to the beat of an hourglass-shaped drum.
It seems I see again the innocent gentleness of country folk and the simple customs of old age.

525.

Yakchŏng Kim, please prepare lunch, and p'unghŏn[296] Yi, please prepare wine and side dishes.
Tangjang Wu, please bring musicians for the six-string zither, twelve-string zither, two-string fiddle, five-string mandolin, flute, pipe, and hourglass-shaped drum.
I'll take care of the writing, singing, and bringing gisaengs.

526.

The red silk skirts of Pyŏngyang gisaengs, the indigo silk skirts with moon and flower patterns of Uju gisaengs.
The brown cotton slip and apron with the same colored strings of Yŏnghae and Yŏngdŏk gisaengs.
I'm afraid we'll be like them if we keep living like this.

527.

---

[292] Head of the district compact.
[293] An executive of the district compact.
[294] Officer for the Encouragement of Agriculture.
[295] Village headman.
[296] A man in charge of matters for a district or a town.

White gulls fly over the Taedong River and tall green pines lean over the Ch'ŏngnyu Cliff.
Twilight shines aslant on the dot-like mountains in the wide eastern field, and I will float in a fishing boat on the overflowing waters north of Changsŏng.
I will take a gisaeng, get dead drunk, and sail up and down from Mt. Kŭmsu to Nŭngna Island, following the tide.

528.

I climbed to Hanbyŏk Pavilion after the rain stopped to take in the view—the high attic, a stream, flowers, and the moon.
Many beautiful women, and music ringing in the sky. A magnificent sight and a rowdy banquet.
Boy, fill my cup. A traveler from a distant land wants to wash away his worries.

529.

When I enter Wansan[297] and climb to Man'gyŏng Pavilion, the spring landscape is at its peak above the old capitol of Samhan.
A nobleman in silk with a gisaeng, wine, side dishes, and a paeksŏlga[298] tune with wind and string accompaniment.
Today I enjoy a great man's pleasures and a place famous for its beauty.

530.

---

[297] Chŏnju's old name. Samhan refers to the Three Han States, and Wansan was the capital of the Later Packche.
[298] A song frequently sung when people with the same taste exchange poems.

Boys herding cows on a green hill thick with willow trees,
When people catch all the fish in the front and back streams and put them in the basket, please bring them to us on the backs of your cows.
I'm afraid we can't take them with us, we're in a hurry.

531.

Flat brown seaweed, did you see the rockweed leave?
Angry, it opened wide its taro-like eyes and, wearing sweet laver for shoes, pushed against the tiny brown seaweed to walk up the street of kelp.
At any rate, it went away, betraying no anger on its red algae[299]-like face.

532.

Hi there, please buy tongnanjii.[300] Merchant, what do you call this? I'll buy it.
The hard outer shell, the soft flesh inside, two eyes moving back and forth, eight small moving legs, two big legs, green marinated crab and black marinated crab, please buy this marinated crab, which crunches with every bite.
Merchant, don't ramble on so much. Just say marinated crab.

533.

Young lady, whether you become my concubine or I become your paramour,
We're like butterflies that find a flower, geese that find water, spiders chasing what's caught in a web, cormorants that find

---

[299] Its exact scientific name is *Peyssonnelia caulifera Okamura* 1899
[300] Pure Korean word for soy sauce marinated crab.

fish, chopsticks to the eggplant, spoons to the watermelon.
You're an ironsmith's daughter, and I'm a caster. After casting one pot, I'll use the remaining iron to cast another.

534.

The twice-ninety-nine-year-old[301] man is drunk on filtered wine.
Boys, don't laugh at him as he totters and staggers left and right in the wide street.
It feels like only yesterday when I had a youthful heart.

535.

Hi there, please buy this firewood. Merchant, how much is your firewood?
A mal[302] of bush clovers and five does[303] of dried grass and leaves. So one mal and five does. Please buy them and give them a try. They burn well.
If you make one fire with them, you'll always want to buy them.

536.

Korean mandolin, why do you grumble wherever you go?
How can I not grumble when people coil my slender neck and pluck my belly with a wintry scallion-like hand?
Perhaps you're the only instrument that produces the sound of large and small balls falling on the jade tray.

537.

---

[301] This hyperbole emphasizes his old age.
[302] Traditional unit of measure, about 18 liters.
[303] Traditional unit of measure, a doe is about 1.8 liters.

Puryakkŭmi,[304] geese, and ducks float aimlessly on the boundless water.
Reeling mandarin ducks and bustards and cranes floating aimlessly, are you enjoying the water, whether or not you know its depths?
Eyeing another's lover, I'm at a loss not knowing his depths.

538.

Spinning hemp, I twisted threads together,
Which snapped in the middle. I licked it, running it through my white teeth and red lips, holding both ends in my slender hands, trying to piece the thread back together.
Alas, I will join together like hemp threads when my life comes to an end.

539.

The auspicious spirit of Mt. Nam is luxurious and the waters of the Han River overflow.
Our king will enjoy a long life in a peaceful reign until the mountain crumbles and the river dries up.
And we, his people, sing Kyŏgyangga[305] in this peaceful reign.

540.

I think my love is the white fox fur cloth of Lord Mengchang[306]

---

[304] A kind of waterfowl. Details are unknown.
[305] Ground Thumping Song, 擊壤歌, sung by old men to praise Emperor Yao's peaceful reign.
[306] Lord Mengchang, born Tian Wen, was an aristocrat and statesman of the Qi kingdom in ancient China, one of the famed Four Lords of the Warring States period.

in a cold winter.
But my love thinks I'm the coarse comb of a toothless old
 monk in the Chunghŭng Temple on Mt. Samgak.
I hope Heaven appreciates my lonely immersion in unrequited
 love and makes it mutual.

541.

I'd like to make a window nowhere else but in my breasts.
I'd like to make a window in my breasts, using a claw hammer
 to install an attic screen door, a finely-threaded screen door,
 a screen door that lifts, a hinged door, a female stone hinge,
 a male stone hinge, and an eyebolt.
When my heart is heavy, I will open and close that window.

542.

To travel into the sky looking for my love on a cold, snowy day,
I take off my shoes and socks to hold them in my hands,
 against my breasts, tossing and turning, flying quickly up
 into the sky, lightly, without stopping.
My bare feet aren't cold but my breasts have gooseflesh, even
 when I pull my clothes up.

543.

While I was complaining about how hard it is to wait for
 someone, the cock crowed three times before dawn.
I went out to see ten thousand layers of green mountains and
 the green waters meandering by.
At last my love showed up on a white horse with a barking dog.
 My happiness knew no bounds. Our mutual pleasure will be
 endless tonight.

544.

When the spring wind blows, I use a stick to climb Mt. Nam and see Seoul's topography.
Mt. Inwang and Mt. Samgak support the North Pole, like a tiger and a dragon. A golden rope ties together Mt. Nam and the Han River. Seoul will last for up to ten million years.
Our king cultivates virtues, his subjects take care of state affairs, and this courteous Eastern country[307] enjoys the world of Emperor Yao and Shun.

545.

On the curved bough of the tall exuberant pine trees on Mt. Paekhwa
Grows a strange bump—wide, long, knotted— caused by pine gall rust. I hope my beloved's tool[308] is like that, not smooth.
Only if it's just like that, I won't mind even if I live in nakedness, hungry.

546.

If he has Shichong's riches and Du Mu's demeanor, which is rewarded with many oranges,
What good is it if his tool is poor when he works at night—I'll dream it better in a dream.
Poor as he is, with nothing special about him, he'll be my beloved if his tool weighs enough to match mine.

547.

---

[307] Refers to the Chosŏn dynasty.
[308] A metaphor for a penis.

I've raised dozens of dogs, none more hateful than this one.
When someone I hate visits, it wags its tail, jumps up and down,
    runs forward to greet him, but when my beloved comes, it
    wriggles, steps back and forth, growls to drive him away.
Spoiled rice overflows many bowls, but I will never feed you.

548.

Cricket, cricket, poor is the cricket.
Why does it chirp all night starting at moonset? Its every note,
    long or short, is sad and awakens a woman from a light sleep.
Leave it alone. It's an insignificant creature, but it understands
    my heart.

549.

Even if people drill a round hole in my heart, loosely twist a
    lefthanded straw rope
To put it into the hole and pull it briskly from both ends, I'll
    endure it as many others do.
But I won't make it, if someone asks me to live alone, apart
    from my love.

550.

Bitch with a beautiful face and a dirty heart, even your pussy is
    unfaithful.
How can you say, "Please stay with me tonight," having already
    promised to meet a young man at twilight?
Leave her be. Why should I blame her when a gisaeng without
    a master and prodigal men enjoying spring flowers think the
    same way?

551.

A red ant with a broken back, boils on its front legs, and sores on its hind legs
Traveled over Samjae Pass in Kwangnŭng, bit a tiger in the waist, lifted it up, and crossed the North Sea.
My love, my love, figure things out for yourself, despite what others say.

552.

Even a monk is a man, and I miss him after sleeping with him.
I rested my head on his headgear made of usnea, he put his head on my headpiece. I covered my body with his robe, and he covered himself with my skirt. Asleep, I realized our love became one with the headgear and headpiece.
When I thought of that the next day, I couldn't calm my pounding heart.

553.

Sigh, a feeble sigh, through which gap did you come?
I installed an attic screen door, a finely-threaded screen door, a sliding door, a hinged door, a female stone hinge, a male stone hinge, an eyebolt, and locked it tightly with a turtle- and dragon-shaped lock. Did you fold them like screens or roll them up like scrolls? Through what gap did you come?
Anyway, I can't fall asleep on nights when you come.

554.

I respect Bai Juyi's[309] artistic taste.[310] Swift horses and lovely women are every man's desire.

---

[309] A renowned Chinese poet and Tang dynasty government official.
[310] Refers to the taste for flowers, wine, the moon, and friends.

When we moved in my old age, our family was three—my wife, son, and me. I loaded a crane, a geomungo, and books onto a boat—I wanted to maintain my fidelity and retire cleanly.
The names of the Tang dynasty's three greatest writers, including Li Bai and Du Fu, should shine forever. How can it not??

555.

A pair of geese flying in the sky, will you stop by the palace in Seoul?
Please deliver my news to my love when you fly from here to there, and news of my love to me when you fly from there to here.
"We're on our way to see our lovers and don't know if we'll deliver it or not."

556.

Liu Bei with great generosity and talented Zhuge Liang, who helped the king without showing anger and joy, surpass figures from the three dynasties.[311]
With the help of the five general's[312] dauntless power, they attacked the fortresses, occupied lands. Their high fidelity and loyalty to the king was unrivaled,
But Heaven did not help them unite the three nations—the heroes' grudge is still felt even one hundred generations later.

557.

---

[311] Refers to the three ancient dynasties of Xia, Yin, and Zhou.
[312] Refers to General Guan Yu, Zhang Fei, Zhao Yun, Ma Chao, and Huang Zhong, who helped Liu Bei.

Who loathes such a good thing as sex?
King Mu of Zu was a son of Heaven, but he indulged in the feast at Yaochi. Though Xiang Yu was a man of great strength, he sang sadly when the autumn moon shone on the camp. Emperor Xuanzong of Tang was an excellent ruler, but he also wept on leaving Yang Guifei.
How, then, can a petty man like me not do what I should do and grow old in vain, foolishly expecting to live for a hundred years?

558.

King of Kings, please act on this humble wish of mine:
A huge amount of wine remains without an owner. Please investigate why this is so and issue a formal document allowing me to do what I intend to do.
"I have thoroughly investigated what you said in your petition. If no land or land tax was awarded even to Liu Ling and Li Bai, you cannot dispose of public goods as you like."

559.

I don't fancy a magnificent mansion or silk clothes or steamed white rice.
Gold and silver, servants and farmland, silk skirts, silk long hood, amber decorative knives, a purple top jacket, a toupee, natural dyes—all seem to belong to dream.
What I really want is a handsome young husband who's good at speaking, writing, and in bed.

560.

The broad streets of Changan, spring wind in March, high buildings on the main street, many flowers and fragrant grasses,

An excellent poet at Five Tombs, who was also a chivalrous fighter enjoying wine and leading all the women wearing silk skirts in the peach- and apricot-blossomed streets. While he travelled, dancing and singing along with the band, he took a break to tour our country, enjoying nature in all its beauty, the Buddhist temples, and the lands of the hermits.

In this peaceful reign, the government and civilians work together, and this bright peaceful light is no different from the ancient one, thanks to the Three Sovereigns and the Five Emperors.

561.

Mountains grew massive because they didn't refuse any soil, great rivers and seas became great because they didn't decline any water.

How can I find and make friends with such heroes and talented people as the Eight Sons of Jianan,[313] the Seven Sages of the Bamboo Grove,[314] Li Bai, and Sushi, all men of refined taste, enjoying drinking and excelling at writing poems?

Swallows and sparrows belong to the same family of birds as geese and swans. What's wrong, then, if a mad traveler wandering here and there sits on the lowest seat and enjoys himself at a banquet of talented people?

---

[313] Seems to refer to Jiananqizi, the Seven Sons of Jianan, the famous seven writers during the time of Jianan in the late Han Dynasty—Kong Rong, Chen Lin, Ruan Yu, Xu Gan, Wang Su, Ying Yan, and Liu Zhen. Jian is the reign name of Emperor Xian of Han.

[314] The Seven Sages of the Bamboo Grove were a group of Chinese scholars, writers, and musicians of the third century CE—Ji Kang (also known as Xi Kang), Liu Ling, Ruan Ji, Ruan Xian, Xiang Xiu, Wang Rong, and Shan Tao.

562.

A tiny one-eyed, limping frog, which suffered for three years from piles, stomachache, migraines, and persistent rashes,
Thought it easy to climb up a 150-cha pole. But I don't know how it can climb down.
Now that I have a new lover I also don't know what will happen later.

563.

Ospreys play in pairs on the blue pond, with the bright moon illuminating the window.
Crickets chirp plaintively by the sad silk curtain, only a few people can be seen in the depths of the night, water trickles in the water clock, the incense is almost burned off in the censor, stars lie aslant, and the moon has set. Where is my old beloved? Who seized him?
I don't think he ever gives me a thought, but he's all I think about. Even if I die, my intestines burning with love for him, I'll never forget him.

564.

"When the owl cries at midnight over the Wŏlang rock,
The old people used to say, a young concubine, someone's mistress who plays all sorts of detestable tricks on him, will drop dead."
The concubine says, "Please don't say that. I heard a wife who treats her husband poorly and envies his mistress will die young."

565.

My husband is a dried-bush-clover broom peddler, my
    paramour is a rice-straw broom peddler.
The men I have an eye on are a peddler of clubs to knock, a
    peddler of wooden rollers to roll, a peddler of spinning
    wheels to spin, a peddler of well buckets that rush to the
    well trembling and plunge into it to scoop up water.
With this face, couldn't I find a peddler of strainers wherever
    I go?

566.

There are too many things for a young man to do.
Read books, practice sword fighting and archery, ride a horse,
    enter public office, make friends, drink wine, womanize,
    sing in a good season, all for a magnanimous spirit.
In old age, retreat to nature, plow the field, weed a rice paddy,
    fish, play the geomungo, play Go, play joyfully in the
    mountains and rivers. Comfortable and joyous in my life,
    there is no end to the pleasure I take in this landscape in
    each of the four seasons.

567.

Maktŏk's mother living over the pass, don't brag about your
    daughter.
When she slept a disturbed sleep in my breasts, she gnashed
    her teeth, snorted, farted. I swear it smelled really bad.
    Please take her soon.
Maktŏk's mother rushed out to defend her: "My youngest
    daughter had no illnesses except stranguria, stomachache,
    and what she was born with."

568.

Why doesn't he come? Why can't he come?
"Did someone build a fortress with cast iron on the road home, add walls inside the fortress and a house inside the walls and put a wooden grain chest in the house and a box inside the chest and tie you up and put you in the box and lock its double eyebolts with a dragon- and turtle-shaped lock? Is that why you don't come to me?"
A month has thirty days, so shouldn't be there at least one day you visit?

569.

His face is pitted and dark with large whiskers. Even his dick is fat and long.
He isn't young but climbs on top of me every night. When he sticks his big tool into my tiny hole and moves back and forth, not only love but Mt. Tai seems to press down on me. To the sound of farting I have to summon the strength with which I suckled my mother's breast.
What bitch would envy that concubine even if someone takes that guy to live with and he never returns?

570.

When spring was in full bloom in Luoyang, every tree and blade of grass was joyful.
I climbed Paegundae Peak[315] to the Munsu Temple and the Chunghŭng Temple[316] with five or six adults and seven or eight children, the sky came near, encircling Mt. Samgak to the north, thanks to the country's endless reign. As if to

---

[315] The highest peak of Mt. Pukhan in Seoul.
[316] These two temples are located on Mt. Pukhan.

drink Yunmeng[317] from a man's chest, I washed my horsehair hat string in Kuch'ŏn'ŭn Falls[318] and sang to the beat of my feet.

Walking and resting by turns, I came back to Sŏnggyun'gwan,[319] believing I had acquired Zeng Dian's[320] sophisticated taste for enjoying nature.

571.

I will cut the small pine tree at Hansongjŏng Pavilion to make a small boat

And load wine, side dishes, a geomungo, gayageum, a two-string fiddle, a five-string mandolin, a large transverse flute, a flute, an hourglass-shaped drum, a dancing drum, musicians, the best flint of white pebbles from Mt. Anam, a mother-of-pearl decorated tobacco pipe, good tobacco, Kangnŭng gisaengs, and Samch'ŏk gisaengs, and row the boat to Kyŏngp'odae on a bright moonlit night

To get drunk and pole the boat with the tide, climbing up and down the Ch'ongsŏkjŏng Pavilion, Kŭmnan'gul Cave, Yŏngnangho Lake, and Sŏnyudam Lake.

572.

The heart of a pheasant hen chased by a hawk on a mountain cleared of trees and stones,

The heart of the chief boatman who encountered pirates, his

---

[317] One of the seven greatest ponds in the Chu dynasty.
[318] Autumn on Mt. Pukhan.
[319] Royal Confucian Academy.
[320] Zeng Dian, courtesy name Zixi, also known as Zeng Xi, was an early disciple of Confucius.

boat loaded with a thousand sŏk[321] of rice in the middle of the boundless sea, which lost its oars, anchor, sails, and rope, its masts snapped, its helm displaced, the wind blowing, waves crashing, fog thickening, and there are still tens of thousands of li to sail, the four corners darken, the world going blank as a white-capped roller approaches—
How can you compare their hearts with mine? I lost my beloved the day before yesterday.

573.

Mother-in-law, don't roll on the kitchen floor, crying that your daughter-in-law is no good.
Was I a loan or did you pay for me? My father-in-law is bone dry as a branch sprouting from the rotten trunk of a chestnut tree, my mother-in-law is gaunt as sun-dried ox dung, my sister-in-law is sharp as the tip of a new awl in a straw bag woven three years ago, and my husband has bloody stools, intense as a yellow cucumber flowering among the wild millet growing in a field of fine grains.
Why are you so unhappy with your daughter-in-law, flowering bindweed in a fertile field?

574.

Instead of tearing down the hill to fill the narrow street, please demolish the mound to narrow the wide gap.
Instead of saying the neck of a dabchick is unusually long as it flies from Kwanghŭimun Gate over Tumopo, the Han River, Noryang, Tongjak, Yongsan, and Samp'o Rapids, rummaging for food while moving up and down, I wish my tool was so long the gisaengs of government offices large

---

[321] Traditional unit of measure, about 180 liters.

and small would rush out to hold it in their trembling hands.
Only then could I call myself a generous lover.

575.

I send my thoughts to the palace where my king lives, so please judge my appeal.
Gray-Haired Man turns, envied by all the crown-like old men and graying young men, making heroes and talented men the first to go gray. Please investigate his actions and issue orders to prohibit gray hair.
Our heavenly king says, "The right ways of the world are entrusted to Gray-Haired Man. My own hair has also turned gray, and I can't do anything about it. I make no judgement. Therefore do so prudently."

576.

I'll tell, you see, I'll tell, how can I not tell your husband,
Do you want me to tell him how, pretending to draw water, you set the water jar down by the well, hung your round head pad on the jar handle, called out secretly to little Kim, your paramour, grasped his hand tight, and went into the hemp field? I don't know what you guys did there, but small stacks of hemp fell, only the big ones kept dancing.
You, small child, with loose lips! Don't lie. I'm a wife in this village. I only dug up small hemps.

577.

Wearing shoes made from an inner layer of kudzu skin, binding a sack around his back,
With twelve joints of Xiaoxiang dotted bamboo to use as a stick, a man leaves briskly, crossing the mountain ridge, hill,

fields, and a stone path in the mountain. You saw him, didn't you? He's my monk-husband.

Others may call him a monk, but I really like him when he mounts my jade-like breasts around midnight, rubbing his watermelon-shaped head here and there between them.

578.

Ten thousand-gil[322]-high peaks of famous peace-bringing mountains that soar high into the sky, making a golden lotus flower blossom.

A huge wall towers above, taking Mt. Samgak as the chosan[323] to the north and Mt. Nam as the ansan.[324] Mt. Nak is a blue dragon to the left[325] and Mt. Inwang a white tiger to the right.[326] Auspicious light hovers in the sky, resting outside the palace door. So beautiful, how a clean spirit begets talented men. How stable are the mountains and rivers of our country! This is the capital, where the customs and culture of a peaceful reign will long endure.

This is the year of good crops, and our country is peaceful. To see a giraffe playing in autumn leaves and chrysanthemums, I climb Mt. Pugak, eat heartily, get drunk. Wandering here and there, I am moved by our king's benevolence.

579.

Now that they won't let me see him, I certainly won't.

---

[322] A traditional unit of measure, one gil is about 2.4 m.
[323] A high peak on a ridge farthest from the critical spot that shapes one's fortune in geomancy.
[324] A mountain opposite a house or grave in geomancy.
[325] A mountain to the left of the main mountain in geomancy.
[326] A mountain to the right of the main mountain in geomancy.

I'm travelling ten thousand li, the entrance to the harbor is choked off, the North Sea is blocked by the Milky Way, the climate is rough, the raven in the depths of the mountain caws, passing over the base of Mt. T'aebaek. In a land where people can find nothing to eat, not even a stone, and die of hunger, where can I find my love?
Boy, when my beloved comes, don't tell him I starved to death. Say I missed him dearly, suffered vertigo and blurred vision, was all skin and bones. Walking close to the reed railing, I peed, lifting my leg, putting my hand to my brow, and fell to my death.

580.

When I heard that my beloved was on his way, I ate dinner early,
And crossed from the inner gate to the main gate, where I sat on the threshold. With my hand on my brow, I looked at the mountain to see if he was near. Something black-and-white stood there, which I thought was my beloved. I pulled off my socks and shoes, held them to my breasts, and hurried toward him, not caring if the road was dry or wet. When I gave him a sideways glance and warm greetings, I realized I had been fooled by the stalk of hemp I nibbled last July 14th.
Whoops, I was lucky it was night. If it was day, others would have laughed at me.


If writings and verses are published, they will be handed down and endure for even a thousand years. But songs sung at one point in time are forgotten. It is regrettable that they disappear like smoke. I have collected songs by famous people, outstanding scholars, rural commoners, and women from the end of Koryŏ to the present, corrected mistakes, wrote them down and edited them into a book titled *Songs of the Green Hills.* I hope that dilettantes will recite them with their mouths, think about them with their minds, open them with their hands, and look at them with their eyes so that they spread widely.

Namp'anop'o wrote this on May 16, 1728.

## *Postscript*

One day Kim Ch'ŏnt'aek brought me a book titled *Songs of the Green Hills,* saying, "This book has many works by masters and great men, the elders of our nation, but also licentious stories and vulgar words from lowly commoners and the streets, because I collected everything. The songs gathered here are low art, so how can a gentleman not feel hurt seeing them? What do you think, sir?"

I said, "No need to worry. Confucius didn't throw away 'The Odes of Ching' and 'The Odes of Wei' when he edited *Book of Odes,* because he wanted to keep both the good and the evil to encourage and warn people. Why should 'The Cry of the Osprey' be a poem in 'The Odes of Chow and the South' and 'Gengzai'[327] be a song in the time of Emperor Shun? They're good, only if they don't fall too far afield of human nature. Poetry strayed from the old standards after *Book of Odes*. After the Wei and Jin dynasties, students of poetry regarded trafficking in words a good thing and madly decorating things a form of excellence; when they discussed disorderly sounds and methods of beautifying wordings, feeling and emotion disappeared. Harmful effects were more severe in our country. Only songs didn't stray, remaining close to the will of men with taste. They use our own language to express emotions, they move people gently when they're sung. As for the sound of the commoner's songs, the melody is not

---

[327] 賡載 Poetry originated from the ancient practice of exchanging songs, in which a king's subjects would sing back and forth to a song written by the king. Here it refers to the songs Emperor Shun and his vassal Gao Yao 皋陶 exchanged.

refined but pleasing and comfortable, lamenting and resentful, wild and unruly, a rough character deriving from nature's true aspect. If the inspector of the customs of people had received the order to collect them, they should, I suppose, have collected not poems but songs. So how can people say songs are trivial?

He said, "Then please write a postscript for the book." I said, "Sure, I liked listening to songs and especially to your singing. How can I not say a word, after you have collected these songs?" I wrote down what he asked for and gave it to him. Kim Ch'ŏntaek is intelligent. He has taste. He can recite three hundred poems from *Book of Odes*. He's not just a singer.

Maaknoch'o wrote this in late June, 1727.

# Glossary

Akpu 樂府 Yuefu: Chinese poems composed in the style of folk songs; literally, "Music Bureau," a reference to the imperial Chinese government office charged with collecting or writing lyrics.

Ansan: A mountain opposite a house or grave in geomancy

Chahyŏn: The second, thin string of the Korean zither.

Chakchŏgori: An outer jacket and inner jacket worn together. Korean woman used to wear an inner jacket on top of a Chŏksam and an outer jacket over them.

Changgu: Hourglass-shaped double-headed drum.

Chasu: Head of the district compact.

Chingnyŏng: A coat with a straightened collar.

Chin'ogwisaenam ritual: A shamanistic ritual to lead the soul of a dead man to Heaven.

Ch'ojungdaeyŏp 初中大葉: The first chungdaeyŏp tune, the representative music of the 17$^{th}$ century, which in the next century was regarded as a slow tune.

Chŏksam: A Korean-style unlined summer jacket.

Ch'ŏnhyangju: Wine from the world of hermits, which in literary terms means heavenly fragrance.

Ch'ŏngmyŏng: One of the twenty-four divisions of the year on the lunar calendar, around April 5$^{th}$.

Ch'osaktaeyŏp 初數大葉: The first tune of saktaeyŏp, a representative 18th-century tune. The saktaeyŏp tune is faster than the chungdaeyŏp tune.

Chosan: A high peak on a ridge farthest from the critical spot that shapes one's fortune in geomancy.

Chungsŏdang: Another name for the Office of Special Advisers.

Hakch'ang'ŭi: A traditional jacket with wide sleeves and parted seams. A broad black band was attached to the edges of the white cloth.

Hansik: The Day of Cold Food, the 105th day after the winter solstice.

Hyangga: Poems written using Chinese characters in a system known as hyangchal during the Unified Silla and early Goryeo periods of Korean history.

Hyangŭm: An annual ceremony in October performed by Confucian scholars, who then drink together.

Ibukchŏn 二北殿: A variation of pukjŏn. *Han'gŭmsinbo (New Scores for Korean Zither)* notes that it is composed of three movements, while the songs have five.

Ijungdaeyŏp 二中大葉: The second chungdaeyŏp tune, the representative music of the 17th century, which in the next century was regarded as a slow tune.

Isaktaeyŏp 二數大葉: The second tune of the saktaeyŏp, the representative 18th-century tune. The saktaeyŏp tune is faster than the chungdaeyŏp tune.

Kangsin: A meeting of the members of the local kye, a private traditional fund popular among Koreans, who chip in a modest amount of money and take turns receiving shares of it in a lump sum. They usually have a drinking party to strengthen their bonds.

Kosanyusu tune: A tune based on an anecdote concerning Bo Ya and Zhong Ziqi. Bo Ya was good at playing the qin. Zhong Ziqi was good at listening to the qin. When tall mountains inspired Bo Ya's playing, Zhong Ziqi said, "Towering, like Mt. Tai!" When flowing water inspired Bo Ya's playing, Zhong Ziqi said, "How vast are the rivers and oceans!" Whatever Bo Ya thought, Ziqi never failed to grasp it. Bo Ya said, "Amazing! Your heart and mine are the same!" When Ziqi died, Bo Ya broke the strings of his qin and vowed never to play again. Thus the melody of High Mountains Flowing Water.

Kyemyŏn: Traditional Korean musical note. It is melancholy.

Kyori: Fifth Councilor in the Office of Special Counselors, Academy of Talented Scholars, and Office of Diplomatic Correspondence.

Kwŏnnong: The board member of a community association whose duty is to encourage farming.

Mangmak note: The highest among the seven notes of Korean music.

Manhoengch'ŏngnyu 蔓橫淸類: It is a collection of tunes called manhoeng and songs with similar tunes. Manhoeng is the sound of singing songs cunningly. Ch'ŏng means the sound of singing a high note. This is music in the tradition of nong, nak, and p'yŏn, and is used to sing songs with many lyrics.

Naepyŏngjo: An office in the Ministry of War.

Naksijo 樂時調: A sijo tune considered to be endlessly pleasing, like a flower garden on a sunny day, published in a mid-eighteenth-century anthology.

Paeksŏlga: A song frequently sung when people with the same taste exchange poems.

Pip'a: A traditional musical instrument, a pear-shaped five-string mandolin.

Pohŏja 步虛子, Pacing the Void: Tang music introduced during the Koryŏ dynasty, which began as court and private instrumental music during the Chosŏn period.

Pukchŏn 北殿: Song music dating from the Koryŏ dynasty. Most *Scores for Zither Music,* including *Scores of Kŏmun'go,* are composed of three movements, while the songs have five.

P'unghŏn: A man in charge of matters for a district or a town.

Samjungdaeyŏp 三中大葉: The third chungdaeyŏp tune, the representative music of the 17th century, which in the next century was regarded as a slow tune.

Sain 舍人: A drafting adviser in the Office of Special Councilors.

Sinsŏng: Literally, "new voice," referring to saktaeyŏp 數大葉 a popular 18th-century tune.

Sangjikpang: Night duty room in the Naepyŏngjo.

Sangsŏng 商聲, Shangsheng: A scale that depends on shang,

one of the five notes in Chinese music; a sad tune.

Ssangnyuk 雙六: A game of dice played at the beginning of the year and in winter.

Such'an: Fifth Councilor in the Office of Special Counselors.

Taehyŏn: The third, thick string of the six-string Korean zither.

Tangjang: Village headman.

Tapchŏngjŏl: March 3$^{rd}$ (lunar calendar), when people used to go to the fields to walk on the new grass.

Tongnanjii: Korean word for soy sauce marinated crab.

T'ungso: A six-holed bamboo flute, a traditional musical instrument.

Tŭnggojŏl: September 9$^{th}$ (lunar calendar), when people used to climb mountains to enjoy wine and food.

Wu note: The highest note on the Korean pentatonic scale. It is clear and gallant.

Yakchŏng: An executive of the district compact.

Yŏmillak 與民樂, Enjoyment with the People: Music composed during King Sejong's reign. *Song of the Dragon Flying to Heaven* (龍飛御天歌) was sung to this music, which began as court and private instrumental music during the late Chosŏn period.

Yŏp: A tune in which people sing different lyrics at that same time.

# About the Translators

**Won-Chung Kim** is a professor of English literature at Sungkyunkwan University in Seoul, Korea, where he teaches contemporary American poetry, ecological literature, and translation. He has translated sixteen books of Korean literature into English, including *Because of the Rain: A Selection of Korean Zen Poems* and Seungja Choi's *Phone Bells Keep Ringing for Me* (National Translation Award Long List.) He has also translated John Muir's *My First Summer in the Sierra* and H.D. Thoreau's *Natural History Essays* into Korean.

**Christopher Merrill** has published eight collections of poetry, including *Watch Fire*, for which he received the Lavan Younger Poets Award from the Academy of American Poets; many edited volumes and translations; and six books of nonfiction, among them, *Only the Nails Remain: Scenes from the Balkan Wars, Things of the Hidden God: Journeys to the Holy Mountain,* and *Self-Portrait with Dogwood*. He directs the International Writing Program at the University of Iowa.

www.ingramcontent.com/pod-product-compliance
Lightning Source LLC
Chambersburg PA
CBHW022008160426
43197CB00007B/327